DRUG WARS

DRUG WARS

THE BLOODY REIGN OF THE MEXICAN CARTELS

AL CIMINO

ARCTURUS

Arcturus

This edition published in 2014 by
Arcturus Publishing Limited
26/27 Bickels Yard, 151–153 Bermondsey Street,
London SE1 3HA

ISBN: 978-1-78404-014-7
AD004101UK

Printed in China

CONTENTS

INTRODUCTION

Mexico has long had a reputation as a lawless place. In the days of the Wild West, outlaws would hightail it across the border from the United States to avoid capture. It has also had a lengthy association with drugs. The Native Americans living there have used peyote – a spineless cactus containing the psychoactive drug mescaline – for over five thousand years.

Chinese immigrants in the 19th century brought with them opium, which was then exported into the United States. Parts of Mexico also had the perfect climate to grow both opium poppies and marijuana. Fresh

smuggling routes were opened during Prohibition in the 1920s, when Mexican bootleggers would transport alcohol across the border.

During the Second World War, the United States was cut off from the poppy fields of Asia, but needed morphine, derived from opium, for its wounded servicemen. As a result, Mexican farmers were encouraged to grow poppies. The poppy fields there were guarded by soldiers and the growers grew rich, along with the government officials who exported the crop. After the war Mexico's inferior strain of opium was no longer needed, so the trade went

Illegal drugs worth billions of dollars cross the border from Mexico into the United States annually, leaving a trail of death and destruction in their wake. Since the 1980s, some 60,000–100,000 people have died in Mexico as a result of gang violence, but no one knows the exact figure

underground and producers began making heroin, which became fashionable among jazz musicians.

The Beat Generation of writers in the 1950s began to popularize marijuana. In the 1960s and 1970s, the demand for marijuana among young radicals grew rapidly and the Mexican traffickers were happy to supply it.

A Deadly Trade

During the 1980s, the younger generation's drug of choice became cocaine. The Colombian cartels smuggled it across the Caribbean to Florida, where it was distributed out of Miami. When the United States authorities tried to cut off this route they played into the hands of the Mexican traffickers, who smuggled Colombian cocaine along the routes they had already established for the trafficking of marijuana and heroin. At first, the Mexican gangs were paid in cash to transport the cocaine. After that they were allocated a percentage of the shipment, giving the Mexican cartels a foothold in the worldwide cocaine market. Instead of making one or two million dollars a shipment, they were now making twenty or even forty million dollars a time. Soon they controlled 90 per cent of the cocaine entering the United States. This is estimated to be worth anything up to $70 billion a year.

Next there was methamphetamine. In the United States, it is difficult to obtain the precursor chemicals needed to synthesize the drug. That is not a problem in Mexico and small laboratories hidden away in the boondocks produce 80 per cent of the crystal meth sold in the United States.

Coming across the border the other way are guns. Around 70 per cent of the firearms recovered from crime scenes in Mexico originated in the United States. As a result, Mexico has become one of the most dangerous countries in the world.

The Mexican cartels are also involved in human trafficking, the exploitation of immigrants, kidnapping, murder, money laundering and general corruption. Their money and power undermine the legal system and subvert the government. Campaigning politicians and investigative journalists are assassinated with impunity, while the general population is intimidated by the gang members' mindless violence. Much of the killing goes on between rival cartels, who compete over the trafficking routes. They seem to be willing to go to any lengths to maintain their supremacy.

There have been numerous attempts to suppress the cartels and some of the major players have been jailed for long periods. But others go about their business as fugitives, even with a bounty as large as $7 million on their heads. With enough money to bribe politicians, government officials and police chiefs, they seek to use any crackdown to obliterate their rivals.

In 2000, Mexico's president, Vicente Fox, sent federal troops in to suppress the cartels. By 2006 this police action had escalated to an all-out war, with the new president, Felipe Calderón, deploying more than fifty thousand troops and federal police against the gangsters. Although many of the gang leaders were arrested or killed, violence soared. Meanwhile, poorly paid troops and policemen defected to the cartels, taking their weapons and their expertise with them.

Calderón's successor, President Enrique Peña Nieto, promised a lower-profile approach. He aimed to tackle the violence on a local level by setting up a national gendarmerie to take over from the troops. The federal police were also strengthened in order to boost criminal investigations. Nevertheless, the death toll kept rising.

Law and Disorder

In July 2013, the leader of the ruthless *Los Zetas* Cartel, Miguel Ángel Treviño Morales, was captured by Mexican marines and charged with the kidnapping and killing of 265 migrants, along with numerous other charges including murder and torture. However, it is feared that his removal will only lead to more violence, sparking a bloody power struggle and turf war.

As the fighting escalates many fear that Mexico will turn into a failed state. The problem is that no effort is being made to address the real problem – the seemingly insatiable demand for drugs in the United States. When a big drugs bust is made, the traffickers simply use it as an excuse to hike the price.

Mexican farmers can barely make a living growing legal crops. Cheap manufactured goods from China have resulted in the closure of the factories along the border. For a generation of young men, unemployment means that the only opportunity they have in life is to join the local cartel.

Fighting Dirty

The United States cannot hold the line against drugs. Two states – Washington and Colorado – have legalized marijuana, with another twenty-three going some way towards decriminalizing it.

Meanwhile the suppliers south of the border are making so much money they are finding it hard to launder it. Trailers full of small bills have to make their way back into the American banking system so Mexico, as a country, is not even benefiting from the trade.

The only winners here are a handful of ruthless drug lords who are prepared to torture, kill, massacre and maim to stay in power.

They follow the maxim of Niccolò Machiavelli, that it is better to be feared than to be loved. And they are some of the most fear-inducing men on the planet. Their cruelty matches their other excesses and they have taken on the power of the state in Mexico – a battle they are plainly winning. They are even prepared to take on the might of the United States, fighting a covert, if not outright, war with their powerful neighbour. It was no accident that one of the Zetas' top generals, Iván Velázquez Caballero, called himself *El Talibán*.

A trickle of blood leads to the dead body of a taxi driver who was shot as part of a murderous vendetta conducted by death squads in the city of Acapulco in February 2011. At least a dozen people died

MAP OF MEXICO

UNITED STATES OF AMERICA

Tecate
Tijuana
Mexicali
Ensenada
Douglas
El Paso
Tubutama
Agua Prieta
Ciudad Juárez
5
Ojinaga
Houston
3
Piedras Negras
Rio Grande
9
Gulf of California
Chihuahua City
11
Laredo
Nuevo Laredo
Falcon Lake
14
Reynosa
Brownsville
THE GOLDEN TRIANGLE
Los Mochis
Guanaceví
Monterrey
Matamoros
Angostura
Nuevo León
Badiraguato
6
10
Culiacán
1
Soto la Marina
La Paz
Gulf of Mexico
Los Cabos
Mazatlán
Ciudad Victoria
S I E R R A   M A D R E
Nayarit
Guadalajara
Puerto Vallarta
Guanajuato
Ameca
1
12
Ejutla
Morelia
Angangueo
Veracruz
Tepal-catepec
Uruapan
Mexico City
Colima
Apatzingán
Almoloya de Juárez
Cuernavaca
Paraíso
4
Xoxocotla
13
Santa María Ixcotel prison
Isthmus of Tehuantepec
15
Acteal
Atoyac de Alvarez
Acapulco
Santa María Zoquitlán
San Pedro Totolapa
8
7

NORTH PACIFIC OCEAN

States

1 Sinaloa
2 Jalisco
3 Chihuahua
4 Michoacán
5 Sonora
6 Durango
7 Oaxaca
8 Chiapas
9 Baya California
10 Tamaulipas
11 Coahuila
12 Veracruz
13 Tabasco
14 Nuevo León
15 Guerrero

0   200   400kms
0   200   400miles

THE GUADALAJARA CARTEL

The Guadalajara Cartel was formed in Central Mexico in the 1970s by Rafael Caro Quintero, Miguel Ángel '*El Padrino*' Félix Gallardo and Ernesto '*Don Neto*' Fonseca Carrillo. None of the three drug lords was from Guadalajara, capital city of the state of Jalisco on the Pacific coast. But all three had a formidable background in organized crime.

Born in 1952, Caro Quintero came from La Noria in the hills of Badiraguato in the Pacific state of Sinaloa to the north of Jalisco. Badiraguato is the home town of a

Rafael Caro Quintero amassed a multi-billion dollar fortune from drug trafficking. He used to run the biggest marijuana plantation in Chihuahua, employing at least 1,000 people

LEFT *Ernesto Fonseca Carrillo developed the first links with Colombian dealers*

RIGHT *Guadalajara is the home of mariachi music and tequila, but it has recently been hit by a wave of narco crimes, including grenade attacks and blockades by gunmen*

number of leading figures in the Mexican drugs trade, including Pedro Avilés Pérez, a drug lord from the 1960s who was the first to use aeroplanes to smuggle drugs into the United States, and Joaquín '*El Chapo*' Guzmán Loera, who rose to become the head of the Sinaloa Cartel and Mexico's most wanted drug trafficker. Fonseca Carrillo and *El Chapo*'s sidekick Juan José Esparragoza Moreno also came from Badiraguato.

After working as a cowboy, a farm labourer and a truck driver, Caro Quintero left Sinaloa for neighbouring Chihuahua. He began to grow marijuana there on a ranch on the border of Sonora owned by his younger brother Jorge Luis. The family was well established in the trade. Three of his uncles and one cousin were heroin and marijuana traffickers. A shrewd entrepreneur, Caro Quintero converted second-rate Mexican weed into the potent seedless *sinsemilla* favoured by connoisseurs. He took over neighbouring farms and built a plantation named Rancho Búfalo – 'Buffalo Ranch' – that eventually covered 1,344 acres (540 hectares). A thousand *campesinos*, or peasants, worked there and its annual production was valued at $8 billion.

At first, Caro Quintero worked for Avilés Pérez. But in 1978 Avilés Pérez was shot and killed by the federal police – set up, it was thought, by his treasurer Fonseca Carrillo, who had previously been involved in drug trafficking in Ecuador. At the time, with the support of the Drug Enforcement Administration (DEA) and Jimmy Carter's White House, the Mexican government was cracking down on drug traffickers – as well as left-wing insurgents and political dissidents – in Operation Condor. So Caro Quintero and Fonseca Carrillo fled from the border states of Chihuahua and Sonora to Guadalajara, Mexico's second largest city. There they teamed up with Félix Gallardo.

Born in Culiacán, Sinaloa in 1946, Félix Gallardo had trained with Mexico's *Policía Judicial Federal*, or PJF, and had been the bodyguard of the governor of Sinaloa state. His connections gave them protection. They were joined by another former federal policeman, Juan José Esparragoza

After the Mexican Revolution (1910), immigrants from Mexico flooded across the border into the US, bringing marijuana with them. Anti-drug campaigners talked up the Marijuana Menace, which was associated with Mexicans, and by 1931 29 states had outlawed the substance

Moreno – aka *El Azul*, 'The Blue', because his skin was so dark that it was said to appear blue. They made a fortune growing marijuana in huge plantations, paying the *campesinos* who tended the plants just $6 a day.

They also grew poppies to make opium and heroin, but were introduced into an even more profitable business by Juan Ramón Matta Ballesteros, aka Matta Lopez, Matta del Pozo, José Campo and *El Negro*, who was born in 1945 in Honduras. He was arrested at Dulles International Airport outside Washington, DC, with 54 lbs (24.5 kg) of cocaine in 1970. However, he was not convicted of any drug charges, only for passport violations and entering the United States illegally. He then escaped from the minimum security facility at Eglin Air Force Base in Florida.

Returning to Latin America, Matta began transshipping cocaine and reportedly worked as a hit man for Colombia's powerful Medellín Cartel's drug traffickers, as well as running a cocaine-refining laboratory. These activities attracted the attention of the DEA, who tried to entrap him with a sting operation. When this failed, the Mexican authorities jailed him in 1974 for selling 10 kilos of cocaine. He was released after a year. During his time in jail he was thought to have killed two other prisoners.

The Guadalajara Cartel shipped Colombian cocaine into Arizona and southern California. Instead of taking cash for their services, they took 50 per cent of the cocaine, netting around $5 billion a year. Matta also put the Colombians' Cali Cartel in touch with the smaller Sonora Cartel, run by Rafael Caro Quintero's younger brother Miguel, as the route through Central America was now taking over from the Caribbean route that the Colombian cartels had previously used.

In 1977, Matta was arrested in Colombia for possessing 2,586 lbs (1,173 kg) of cocaine and operating two cocaine-refining laboratories. Another 1,763 lbs (800 kg) of cocaine was found on a property he owned north of Bogotá. Then in 1980 he was arrested with 580 kilos of cocaine. Each time he managed to escape a lengthy term of imprisonment.

Matta managed to stay out of jail, and provide cover for the Guadalajara Cartel, because of his connections with the CIA. In 1978 he funded the 'cocaine coup' in Honduras and supported the Contras who opposed the leftist Sandinista government in Nicaragua. Both were important staging posts on the Central American cocaine route.

Matta owned a security company and hired retired military officers as bodyguards. He also owned the Honduran airline SETCO, which supplied the Contras and carried drugs, along with various construction companies and agricultural operations which laundered the estimated $5 million a week he and Félix Gallardo made from drug trafficking. Some $50 million a year was spent on bribes for Latin American officials.

In 1986, Matta was arrested in Colombia. A $2 million bribe got him out of jail. 'The doors opened for me,' he told a Honduran newspaper, 'and I went through them.'

However, the Iran–Contra hearings in Washington dampened the American government's support for the Contras. Matta was arrested and taken to the United States to stand trial for the torture and murder of DEA agent Enrique Camarena. He was also convicted of trafficking and distribution, and was sent to ADX Florence, a Supermax prison in Colorado.

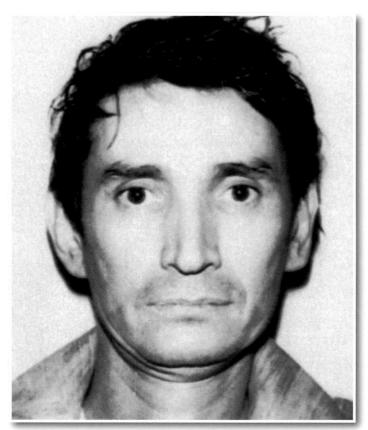

Originally a police officer and governor's bodyguard, Félix Gallardo moved south to Guadalajara in the 1970s when things got too hot up north

Condemned by the Roman Catholic Church, the Cult of Santa Muerte (Holy Death) has millions of followers in Mexico. She is the patron saint of those on the margins of society, including prostitutes, thieves, pickpockets, drug dealers and hit men who pray to her for success. To satisfy some misplaced religious impulse, many in the drug business have built altars to Santa Muerte in their homes

Death of an Agent

Born in 1947 in Mexicali, Mexico and raised in California, ex-United States marine Enrique 'Kiki' Camarena Salazar worked undercover for the DEA. After making major drug busts in the United States, he gained the nickname 'Dark Rooster'. In 1981, he was assigned to the agency's office in Guadalajara where he started Operation Godfather, targeting *El Padrino*, Félix Gallardo. Cruising the backstreets, he picked up tips on the cartel's marijuana-growing operations. However, he also joined Mexican army raids and his face became known.

In late 1984 he was behind the raid on Rancho Búfalo, where 450 Mexican soldiers seized 10,000 tons of marijuana, making it the biggest pot bust in history. Eight times the United States' estimate of Mexico's annual output had been found on one ranch in one day. If that was not bad enough, a vacationing detective spotted some fresh tracks on a Second World War airstrip in Yucca, Arizona. The police set up a roadblock in the desert and seized 700 kilo blocks of cocaine in Christmas tinfoil wrapping.

The Guadalajara Cartel knew nothing of the detective's luck. They decided that the bust had to be an inside job, so Félix Gallardo, Matta and Caro Quintero decided that Camarena was to blame.

Camarena, a Mexican-American agent for the Drug Enforcement Administration, was abducted when he left the US consulate in Guadalajara for a lunchtime date with his wife

On 7 February 1985 Camarena took a break from work to meet his wife for lunch. Not far from the American consulate, a car pulled up and five men jumped out. They identified themselves as Jalisco state cops and told Camarena that '*El Comandante*' wanted to see him. When Camarena told them that protocol required him to notify his office, a jacket was thrown over his head and he was shoved into a Volkswagen van. Meanwhile Alfredo Zavala, the Mexican reconnaissance pilot who had flown Camarena over Rancho Búfalo, disappeared when two men armed with AR-15 assault rifles hijacked the car he was riding in. Neither was seen alive again.

When Camarena did not show up for lunch, his wife contacted the American ambassador, who in turn contacted the Mexican authorities and asked them to start a search. They were slow to respond, so the United States began Operation Camarena, stopping and searching every vehicle coming from Mexico into the United States, and causing a traffic jam at every crossing along the 2,000-mile border from the Pacific to the Gulf.

A month later, on 6 March, the bodies of Camarena and Zavala were found dumped by the roadside some sixty miles (96 km) south of Guadalajara. Both had been beaten to death. Camarena had also been raped. A stick had been forced into his rectum and a blow from a screwdriver had penetrated his skull. Soon after, the DEA was sent a tape recording of his torture session. It was nine hours long. During the brutal procedure he had been given regular injections of amphetamine to prevent him passing out from the pain.

It was clear that the Mexican police had been involved in the abductions. One of them, Primer Comandante Armando Pavón Reyes, the man in charge of the search, was seen at the airport talking to a tall, moustachioed man with thick curly hair. He was wearing black cowboy gear and a lot of gold. Pavón Reyes flashed a badge identifying himself as a member of the Federal Security Directorate – *Dirección Federal de Seguridad* (DFS). The man in black then boarded a Falcon business jet with a number of armed men. As the plane took off, he appeared at the door of the plane, waved an AK-47 at the *federales* and DEA men accompanying Pavón Reyes and shouted: 'Next time, my children, bring better weapons, not toys!' He then took a swig from a champagne bottle and shut the door. The man was Rafael Caro Quintero. It seems that he

Typical street scene in San José, Costa Rica: the killing of DEA agent Camarena stirred up a hornets nest of police activity that brought Comandante Florentino Ventura Gutiérrez over here to a villa where Rafael Caro Quintero was living under an alias

had paid Pavón Reyes a $300,000 bribe to let him escape.

Not wishing to upset the Mexican government, Washington told the DEA to leave the investigation of Camarena's death to the Mexican authorities. It seemed that, to Washington at least, DEA agents were expendable. But the agency was not about to take this lying down.

'Nobody's gonna kill a DEA agent and have some other agency say to us it doesn't matter,' said one former agent.

The DEA then started Operation Leyenda, the biggest homicide investigation ever undertaken. Meanwhile, Pavón Reyes, who had done his best to hinder the search for Camarena, was arrested by Comandante Florentino Ventura Gutiérrez. Another thirteen state and city cops were arrested, one of whom died during interrogation.

While the cops denied any knowledge of Camarena's abduction, torture and murder, Florentino Ventura

quickly discovered that they had been paid off by Caro Quintero and Fonseca Carrillo.

In early April, a phonecall from Caro Quintero's teenage girlfriend Sara Cosio was intercepted. It came from San José in Costa Rica. Florentino Ventura flew there, raided the villa where the pregnant Sara Cosio was staying and arrested a number of Mexicans. One of them, carrying the ID of Marco Antonio Rios Valenzuela, was none other than Rafael Caro Quintero. He was extradited back to Mexico later that day.

Three days later, after a shoot out in a bar in Puerto Vallarta, the police followed a gang back to the holiday home of the chief of police in Ameca, Jalisco. There, surrounded by money and weapons, they found Fonseca Carrillo.

In Mexico City, Caro Quintero and Fonseca Carrillo

signed confessions, but later recanted, saying they had been tortured. Félix Gallardo was the man responsible for Camarena's abduction, torture and death, they said. While Caro Quintero claimed to be in love with Sara Cosio, her parents said she had been kidnapped. He also claimed that he was a philanthropist – that he and Fonseca Carrillo did things for the people that the government hadn't done in ten years.

Nevertheless they were convicted and sentenced to forty years for the murder of Enrique Camarena. Caro Quintero was also convicted for the torture and murder of American writer John Clay Walker and his friend Alberto Radelat,

who had been abducted from a restaurant and killed after Caro Quintero had mistaken them for DEA agents.

At Reclusorio Norte maximum security prison, Caro Quintero and Fonseca Carrillo shared a living area designed to accommodate 600 inmates. They had their own penthouse, complete with soft beds, TVs, VCRs, music, liquor and good food and they didn't have to wear prison uniforms. Every year on his birthday, Caro Quintero would bring the finest Sinaloan bands to play for him and his friends at the prison, with the director's blessing. After four years, though, he was then transferred on through a series of maximum security prisons, where

conditions were harsher. But in August 2013 Caro Quintero was released on procedural grounds because of the objections of the United States government, who immediately asked for his extradition. Fonseca Carrillo was also expected to be released. However, in November, Mexico's Supreme Court overturned the appeals court's decision to release Caro Quintero and ordered his immediate detention. By then, he had disappeared. He remained one of the DEA's five top international fugitives and a $5 million reward was posted for his capture.

Pavón Reyes and another cop were each sentenced to twenty-five years for a raid on a ranch in which five members of a family were killed. It had been staged simply to distract the authorities from the hunt for Camarena. The head of the DFS, thought to have been responsible for the torture of Camarena, was jailed after being arrested in Spain. Four others were convicted of Camarena's kidnapping. One of them, Rubén Zuno Arce, was the brother-in-law of a former president. Charges were also levelled at a Guadalajara gynaecologist for administering the drugs that prolonged Camarena's torture.

Comandante Florentino Ventura, who had led the investigation, was found shot dead in his home in Mexico City along with his wife and his wife's friend. The official story was that, in a drug-fuelled rage, he had shot his wife and her friend, before turning the gun on himself – a likely story!

Troops patrol Puente Grande prison in Jalisco state, from which Caro Quintero was released in 2013 after serving twenty-eight years for the killing of Camarena

Red Ribbon Week

Following the murder of Enrique 'Kiki' Camarena, his high school friend Henry Lozano and Congressman Duncan Hunter started Camarena clubs in local schools. Members wore red ribbons in his honour and pledged to lead drug-free lives. The following year, parent–teacher associations in California, Illinois and Virginia also wore red ribbons and club members were introduced to First Lady Nancy Reagan. In 1988 Congress proclaimed the first Red Ribbon Week as part of a campaign chaired by Mrs Reagan.

On 7 May 1988, Camarena appeared on the front cover of *Time* magazine. *Time* reported:

'Parents who had come together in local coalitions to fight the drug problem took Kiki as their model, embracing his belief that one person can make a difference, and adopting his symbol – the red ribbon – as their own. They began the continuing tradition of wearing and displaying red ribbons as a symbol of intolerance toward the use of drugs.'

The mini-series *Drug Wars: The Camarena Story* won an Emmy in 1990. Since then the Red Ribbon campaign has gone from strength to strength. It is estimated that eighty million people participate in Red Ribbon events each year.

The Acapulco Conference

With the other leaders of the Guadalajara Cartel in jail, Félix Gallardo, who had been living in Culiacán in Sinaloa, moved into a house in an anonymous residential area of Guadalajara, while his wife, mistress and their children occupied another two houses nearby. While still enjoying political protection, *El Padrino* kept a low profile and sought to diversify the cartel, putting it into the hands of lesser-known cohorts who had not been involved in the murder of Camarena.

He convened a conference of Mexico's top narcos in Acapulco and shared out the available *plazas*, as the established drug routes were known. The route through Tijuana went to the two brothers Eduardo and Javier Arellano Félix. While it was reported that they were his nephews, it seems that he had simply known them for a long time while living in Culiacán.

The route through Ciudad Juárez, on the trucking route across Texas, would go to the Carrillo Fuentes family from Guamuchilito, Sinaloa, under the aegis of Rafael Aguilar Guajardo, the federal police commander of the National Security and Investigation Center and an associate of Félix Gallardo. The route through Matamoros, Tamaulipas on the Gulf Coast would remain in the hands of Juan Garcia Ábrego, while Miguel Caro Quintero would continue running the route through Sonora into Arizona.

He could be relied on not to make trouble with the Pacific operation run through Sinaloa to the south. That would be controlled by Joaquín '*El Chapo*' Guzmán Loera and Ismael '*El Mayo*' Zambada García. They brought back into the fold Héctor Luis '*El Güero*' Palma Salazar, who had fallen out with *El Padrino* in the 1970s after the loss of a cocaine shipment. Palma Salazar's accomplice Eduardo '*El Lobito*' had been killed, but Palma Salazar had been spared. They were to smuggle drugs into Arizona and California, while *El Chapo* was also given control over the corridor through Tecate in Baja California.

Félix Gallardo still intended to oversee operations. However, he had not counted on the ambitions of his underlings. On 8 April 1989 he was visiting a friend before a lunchtime appointment with a *Policía Judicial Federal* commander, Guillermo 'Memo' González Calderoni. As *El Padrino* entered the house, five federal agents stormed in after him and pinned him to the ground. When González Calderoni arrived, Félix Gallardo asked: 'What's going on, Memo?'

González Calderoni replied: 'I don't know you.'

Félix Gallardo offered $5 million for his freedom, but González Calderoni was under strict orders from President Carlos Salinas de Gortari, who was attempting to cement his relationship with Washington.

Félix Gallardo was charged with the murder of Camarena, drug smuggling, racketeering and other

ABOVE *The view over El Paso looking towards Ciudad Juárez on the Mexican side. This is the beginning of the trucking route across Texas*

RIGHT Forbes *magazine described Joaquín 'El Chapo' Guzmán Loera as 'the 10th-richest man in Mexico' and 'the biggest druglord of all time'*

violent crimes and was sentenced to forty years.

El Padrino continued to run the trafficking operation from jail using a mobile phone. On the wall of his well-appointed apartment above the warden's office he had a large framed photograph of himself with Pope John Paul II. He also had a large library, being an avid reader, and was a patron of artists including José Luis Cuevas and Martha Chapa. However, these indulgences stopped when he was sent to the Altiplano maximum security prison at La Palma, 50 miles (80 km) west of Mexico City.

There he sought to revenge himself upon *El Güero*, who had been one of his loyal lieutenants. It seems that he blamed him for his downfall. He paid Venezuelan drugs trafficker Rafael Enrique Clavel, Palma Salazar's former business partner, to seduce *El Güero*'s wife. Clavel carried her off to Venezuela, together with her two kids. After forcing her to withdraw $7 million from the couple's bank account, he cut her head off and mailed it back to Palma Salazar in a hatbox. Then he killed the two children by dropping them off a bridge. *El Güero* retaliated by killing Gallardo's lawyer and Clavel's three children.

The Colombian Drug Cartels

The Mexican drug cartels first rose to prominence through trafficking cocaine from the Colombian cartels. Gradually, as the Colombian cartels were crushed, the Mexican cartels took over.

The Colombians had started out trafficking marijuana into the United States, but in the mid-1970s they found it was easier and more profitable to traffic cocaine. It was less bulky and cocaine that could be produced for around $1,500 a kilo in jungle laboratories could be sold on the streets in the United States for as much as $50,000 a kilo.

The Medellín Cartel was founded by José Gonzalo Rodríguez Gacha, a small-time trafficker with roots in the emerald trade, and the Ochoa brothers – Juan David, Jorge Luis and Fabio Ochoa Vásquez – the sons of a wealthy rancher and restaurant owner. Their leader was the violent street thief Pablo Emilio Escobar Gaviria, who had begun his criminal career stealing gravestones. Marijuana smuggler Carlos Enrique Lehder Rivas persuaded them that they could make more money flying cocaine directly into the United States on small planes.

The huge profits were reinvested in better laboratories and better planes. They even took over Norman's Cay, an island in the Bahamas, expelling the population and barring holidaymakers from using it as a trans-shipment and fuelling point. At its height, the Medellín Cartel was bringing in $60 million a day. Pressure from the United States government to extradite the traffickers led to open warfare between the cartels and the Colombian government. Escobar was thought to be responsible for the murder of hundreds of government officials, police officers, prosecutors, journalists, judges and innocent bystanders.

Lehder was captured in 1987 and extradited to the United States, where he was sentenced to life imprisonment without parole, plus 135 years. Rodríguez Gacha killed himself with a grenade during a shoot out with the police that had already claimed the life of his son. The Ochoa brothers surrendered to the authorities, in exchange for light sentences. They each served five years in jail in Colombia, but Fabio was arrested again in a drugs raid and extradited to the United States, where he was sentenced to thirty years.

Escobar also gave himself up in exchange for a reduced sentence and incarceration in a luxurious private prison. When he continued his criminal activities from jail, the authorities sought to move him and he escaped. A massive manhunt ensued. After sixteen months on the run, he was cornered and killed.

The downfall of the Medellín Cartel was partly due to their rivalry with the Cali Cartel, who supplied the Colombian police and the DEA with information on Escobar's whereabouts, as well as directly targeting Escobar and his lieutenants.

Formed in the southern city of Santiago de Cali by the Rodríguez Orejuela brothers, Gilberto and Miguel, and José Santacruz Londoño, the Cali Cartel members were less violent and flashy. Again graduating from smuggling marijuana to cocaine, they invested their profits in legitimate businesses. They also used their money to pay for police protection and, it was alleged, to fund the election campaigns of leading politicians.

Eventually, despite all the precautions they took, they were tracked down. Having seemingly made a deal with the authorities for reduced sentences, the Rodríguez Orejuela brothers were later extradited to the United States where they were sentenced to thirty years. Santacruz Londoño was also arrested, but escaped and was

shot and killed in Medellín while on the run.

After the destruction of the Medellín and Cali Cartels, the Colombian cocaine business fragmented into smaller groups which were less vulnerable to the Colombian authorities and the DEA.

Instead of shipping drugs directly to the United States, they sent the cocaine to Mexico for the cartels there to take it over the border.

Pablo Escobar with Jorge Luis Ochoa: the Mexican drug cartels rose as the Colombian ones sank

THE GULF CARTEL

The oldest of the Mexican crime syndicates, the Gulf Cartel was founded in the 1930s by Juan Nepomuceno Guerra, who had smuggled alcohol across the border during Prohibition. When Prohibition ended in 1933, he set up a crime syndicate called *el cártel de Matamoros* in his home town of Matamoros in the Gulf state of Tamaulipas, directly across the Rio Grande from Brownsville, Texas. The syndicate continued smuggling contraband across the border, but also diversified into prostitution, gambling, gun-running, protection and car theft.

LEFT *A villainous gathering, featuring Juan Nepomuceno Guerra ('Godfather of Matamoros', in white hat), Juan García Ábrego (standing) and Oscar Malherbe (with Ábrego's hand on his shoulder)*

BELOW *The Rio Grande runs from Colorado to the Mexican Gulf and, below El Paso, doubles as the US–Mexico border for a while*

Juan García Ábrego is led out of the FBI office in Houston in 1996

Nepomuceno Guerra coached his nephew Juan García Ábrego in the art of stealing cars. In the mid-1970s, García Ábrego began exporting marijuana into Texas, Louisiana and Florida and by the early 1980s the cartel had begun trafficking cocaine.

García Ábrego built his empire in traditional style, by eliminating his rivals or forcing them to cut him in on their business. In 1984, he ordered the murder of rival dealer Casimiro 'Cacho' Espinosa, who was ambushed and shot, but survived. At dawn the next day, gunmen in combat gear burst into the private hospital where Espinosa was recuperating. During their ten-minute stay, they loosed off three hundred rounds, killing a guard, a bedridden 35-year-old woman, a husband and son who were visiting and Espinosa's sister. Espinosa himself emerged from the attack unscathed, but died a few days later from the wounds he had sustained in the original attack.

Another rival was cut down on International Boulevard in Brownsville in 1991. Brownsville Police Department kept a picture of his black bullet-riddled Chevrolet Blazer on a wall in their headquarters.

At first, the Gulf Cartel was charging the Cali Cartel $1,500 a kilo to transport cocaine across the border. García Ábrego renegotiated the deal, demanding 50 per cent of the cocaine for guaranteed delivery.

'It was a partnership,' Tony Ortiz, one of García Ábrego's primary United States distributors, testified. 'The Colombians would deliver four thousand kilos into Mexico. We split: two thousand kilos for them, two thousand kilos for us.'

President Salinas following his election victory in 1988: he and the Institutional Revolutionary Party (PRI) ruled until 1994, but many blamed him for the increasing power of the drug cartels and the corruption that festered within his administration

His promise of guaranteed delivery meant he had to warehouse the drugs in case a shipment was intercepted. With hundreds of tons stockpiled, García Ábrego could begin his own distribution network, whose tentacles reached as far as New York.

According to *The New York Times*, García Ábrego took over the running of the cartel from his uncle in 1987, when Colombian cocaine was flooding Matamoros and outside traffickers were trying to muscle in.

García Ábrego's ascent was exemplified by one shocking incident. On 27 January 1987, Tomás Morlet Borquez, a former policeman turned international drug trafficker, visited García Ábrego in the Piedras Negras, Nepomuceno Guerra's restaurant in Matamoros. Morlet had spent twenty-two years in the DFS and had been arrested as a suspect in the Camarena murder. Words were exchanged and Morlet ended up dead in the doorway of the restaurant with two bullets in his back and was left to bleed to death. One of García Ábrego's aides was also dead.

'That was when García Ábrego took over,' an American law enforcement official told *The New York Times*. 'It took guts to take out a man like Morlet.'

Nepomuceno Guerra retired to the Piedras Negras, where he told a reporter that apart from a few weeks' imprisonment for tax evasion in 1991 he had never spent more than a few hours in jail. This was reputedly because he had bought off mayors, governors, police commanders and customs officials – all skills that he passed on to his nephew, who paid out millions of dollars in bribes to government officials, including a deputy attorney general.

By 1990, drugs money flooding into the country saturated the administration of President Salinas. The Mexican daily paper *El Financiero* claimed that during the Salinas years – 1988 to 1994 – up to 95 per cent of those working in the attorney general's office had been bribed by the drug cartels. When Salinas picked Javier Coello Trejo, who referred to himself as 'the Iron Prosecutor', as his drug czar, his choice was praised by the United States. However, Eduardo Valle, an investigator in Coello Trejo's own office, said that his boss was on the payroll of García Ábrego to the tune of more than a million dollars a year. Another of Coello Trejo's aides also pocketed more than $50 million from the drugs trade, according to Valle. As a result the office's drug enforcement operations tended to focus on the Gulf Cartel's rivals.

In 1994, García Ábrego's cousin and accomplice in cocaine trafficking, Francisco Pérez Monroy, testified in a Texas drug trial that he had personally delivered money and gifts to the deputy attorney general and his wife.

'The suits and the money,' he told the court, 'they were so that he wouldn't be bothered by the movement of drugs.'

No one seemed to be bothered about Coello Trejo's drug connections. He only found himself in hot water when four of his bodyguards were convicted of raping nine women in Mexico City. Under pressure from religious groups, he was forced to resign.

'This is a blow,' a state department official told the *Los Angeles Times*.

But his talents did not go unused for long. In 1995, he was serving as an adviser to Mexico's new internal security apparatus, the *Coordinación de Seguridad Pública de la Nacíon*, according to the Mexico City newspaper *La Reforma*.

García Ábrego also took the cartel into the business of money laundering. Two American Express employees in Brownsville were indicted for laundering $30 million for him. Seventy members of the cartel were convicted and $53 million was seized, while García Ábrego was indicted in Houston, but remained a fugitive.

The Fish

Tony Ortiz was nicknamed *El Pescado* because he had once owned a fish market in Houston. He also ran one of the Gulf Cartel's longest-running distribution cells because he was very careful. No one knew where he lived because he always met associates in hotels such as La Quinta on the Southwest Freeway, never at his home. He didn't have a phone and could only be contacted via a pager under the name of 'Mohammed'. And he never touched the cocaine himself.

'It is too much of a risk,' he said. 'When I can pay somebody else, why take the chance?'

He had started trafficking marijuana on his own account in 1979. In the early 1980s, he met Luis Medrano and sold pot for him too. When Medrano joined the Gulf Cartel, Ortiz was employed to transport the cocaine from the Rio Grande Valley up to Houston. He did this by stashing the drugs on the Immigration and Naturalization Service buses that took illegal immigrants caught in the valley to Houston airport to be deported. The INS buses were never stopped at checkpoints and were waved on.

However, one of Ortiz's accomplices, a former INS officer named Joe Polanco, was arrested in 1990 when he was staying in an apartment belonging to Ortiz in Houston. A cautious man, Ortiz moved to San Antonio and dropped out of sight. He continued trafficking using commercial freight companies to carry the drugs, packaged to make them look like legitimate goods. Again this was done through subordinates, so his name never appeared on the shipping documents.

He also used front companies such as A-OK Transmissions in Harlingen and J and T Plumbing Fixtures. A-OK had a warehouse where bricks of cocaine were packed in metal containers that were padlocked or welded shut, then encased in wood. They were then driven over to a legitimate freight company who would ship them to Houston or elsewhere, not knowing what was inside. Sometimes the cocaine was packed in freezers, to disguise the scent. From Houston, the drugs went on to New York, New Jersey or Chicago.

Arrested in 1993, Ortiz was convicted of drug smuggling and was sentenced to six years in jail.

Rich List

The Gulf Cartel's web of corruption easily transferred to the administration of Ernesto Zedillo Ponce de León when he became president in 1994. By then, the DEA estimated that García Ábrego was making as much as $10 billion a year profit. *Fortune* magazine put him on its rich list with an estimated worth of $15 billion. Eventually the Gulf Cartel was pulling in $2 billion a year, according to United States prosecutors.

García Ábrego bought ranches all over Tamaulipas and Nuevo León to the west and private planes would fly him to horse races in southern Mexico. Otherwise he would be with friends in the restaurant of the Drive Inn in downtown Matamoros, surrounded by gold wallpaper and drinking Chivas Regal. He would be wearing an aristocrat's white linen jacket, earning him the nickname *La Muñeca* – 'The Doll' – for his snappy dressing. His other nicknames were *El Paciente*, *El Se* and *El Director* – 'The Patient', 'The Him' and 'The Principal'.

The cartels' hold over Matamoros became so brazen that when a gunman shot a municipal policeman dead in the street for giving him a parking ticket, the local media largely ignored the crime. Months later, a junior reporter named Oscar Trevino mentioned the incident in a year-in-review piece. The publisher ordered the story to be killed but due to a mix-up in the newsroom it was printed. Trevino was then summoned to a restaurant by the publisher to apologize to Mr García Ábrego in person. He was wise to do so. In 1986, García Ábrego had been upset by something he had read in *El Popular*, the largest-circulation paper in Matamoros. Gunmen waited outside the newspaper's office. When the editor Ernesto Flores and reporter Norma Morena left, they shot up their car, then finished each of the journalists off with a bullet in the face.

The violence grew so bad that in 1991 one of García Ábrego's hired gunmen, Armando Barrera, took refuge over the river in Brownsville. In a sworn deposition, he said that García Ábrego had ordered the murder of his brother and thirty-five other people. Most were shot, Barrera said, but others were tortured, burned alive or tied up and thrown into a river. Soon after making these accusations, Barrera himself was gunned down.

García Ábrego was not above turning on his own men. When Tomás 'Gringo' Sánchez, another boss of the cartel, ordered the murder of a Colombian trafficker in a jail in Matamoros, it sparked a prison riot which resulted in the deaths of two cartel members. But García Ábrego had not authorized the hit and Sánchez had brought unwanted attention to the cartel, so he was killed.

No one was safe. García Ábrego was also thought to be behind the assassinations of presidential candidate Luis Donaldo Colosio and the head of Mexico's ruling party, José Francisco Ruiz Massieu.

Shipments

Normally García Ábrego would remain above the fray. He was nowhere to be seen when the drug shipments were handled. This was done from Soto la Marina, a small town about a hundred miles (160 km) south of Matamoros, where the transshipments were handled by Carlos Reséndez, a former *comandante* in the Tamaulipas state police force.

Cocaine was flown into the airstrip packed in cans that were supposed to carry spare gasoline for the planes. When empty they were refilled with gasoline, so the planes could make it home. The cocaine was then put into duffel bags and flown in Cessna 206s to the ranches García Ábrego owned along the Rio Grande around Matamoros.

Future Mexican president Ernesto Zedillo attends the funeral of Luis Donaldo Colosio, whose presidential campaign he had run. Ábrego was said to be behind the assassination

Óscar Malherbe de Léon after his arrest on drug charges in Mexico City in 1997

The operation was overseen by two of García Ábrego's lieutenants – Luis Medrano and Óscar Malherbe de León, a hit man who was credited with at least ten homicides. Both had worked for *Cacho* Espinosa before García Ábrego's bloody takeover. They operated out of a walled compound in Matamoros, patrolled by six to eight armed men.

There was little to worry about, from the police at least. According to the book in which García Ábrego recorded his business expenses, as well as paying off Coello Trejo he was also bribing Emilio López-Parra, a *comandante* with the Federal Judicial Police in Matamoros, and Luis Esteban García Villalón, an agent with the Federal Ministry. They were paid $1.5 million a month just to look the other way.

When a major shipment was ready, García Ábrego would listen out for a pre-arranged message over the radio, recalling all the agents in the field to headquarters for a meeting. Once the area was clear, the cocaine would be taken down to the Rio Grande in pick-up trucks and floated across the river on rafts. On the other side, the drugs would be hidden in safe houses the cartel had set up along the Rio Grande Valley. One of them was a modest white bungalow in Harlingen, Texas. Department of Public Safety officers found nine tons of cocaine packed in duffel bags, flour sacks and cardboard boxes stored there. It was the second largest seizure of cocaine in history. But such finds were rare. It was alleged that cartel money had also been used to pay off officials within the United States too, but north of the border the traffickers usually operated by stealth.

The Gulf Cartel's distribution network within the United States was set up as small cells of individuals, who trusted one another like a guerrilla army or a network of spies. Low-level employees in the distribution system were often arrested, but they could not implicate anyone outside their cell. They would only know the first name or the nickname of the person they were working for. And only the cell leaders would have any contact with anyone in Matamoros.

Gringo

The danger of this arrangement was that García Ábrego's men had little control once the merchandise was on the other side of the border. They fell prey to Tomás Sanchez González, aka *Gringo*. He had started as a lowly loader in Houston and had worked his way up to supervising the cartel's dealers in New York. Then he siphoned off $8 million of the profits and tried to go into business on his own. But the cocaine he had bought with the cartel's money was lost in a bust. *Gringo* paid with his life, killed, it was thought, on the orders of Luis Medrano.

At the peak of his career, *Gringo* had overseen a business that made tens of millions of dollars a week. When the police raided the cartel's warehouse in Queens, they found a furniture van containing a cache of weapons and two dozen U-Haul boxes marked 'Gogrin' – an anagram of *Gringo* – which contained $18.3 million in United States currency. An account book found on Long Island showed that several million dollars were sent back to Houston – then on to Matamoros – every couple of days. Tony Ortiz said he once unloaded $24 million from a tractor-trailer in Houston, but during his time in trafficking he had no idea how many millions he had sent to Matamoros. On another occasion Bill Hoffman, an American working for García Ábrego, picked up $18 million from a series of safe houses in Queens and drove it back to Matamoros in a Chevrolet Suburban.

Money Trouble

These huge amounts of money were a problem for the Gulf Cartel. They could hardly put it into a bank in the United States as all American financial institutions had to report any cash transaction of over $10,000 to the federal government. It was also illegal to take more than $10,000 in cash out of the country without informing United States Customs.

García Ábrego's way round this was to pay Mexican Customs officials to drive the cash over the border for him. This was not foolproof. Two officials were caught driving across the Gateway International Bridge – one of the four bridges that connect Brownsville to Matamoros – in a Jeep Cherokee Wagoneer carrying $2.4 million. But most did not get caught. Then the money was deposited in Mexican banks, in the accounts of front companies set up under the names of various members of the García Ábrego family.

Another way of handling large amounts of cash in small bills was to run a chain of currency exchange houses, or *casas de cambio*, and mix the cash in with the legitimate money.

García Ábrego employed Ricardo Aguirre to run this side of the business. Formerly a gas station manager, he was known as 'Kenny Rogers' because he was always wearing cowboy outfits. Employees would cross the borders in cars or private planes and bring back the cash, filling in all the appropriate forms declaring how much they were carrying. Several million dollars a day would be arriving this way.

The money would then be deposited in the *casa de cambio* account at First City Bank in McAllen, Texas. From there, it would be wired to Banker's Trust in New York. An employee named Antonio Giraldi would then move the money into a number of Swiss bank accounts. García Ábrego was interested in horse racing so one of these was named Stallion investments. It was owned by Aguirre and two relatives, while White Horse Investments was owned by Aguirre, another relative and María del Carmen Olivella – García Ábrego's wife. Both companies were based in the Cayman Islands.

In 1990, Giraldi moved to American Express where he opened an account for Green Mountain Holdings. Over $25 million made its way from First City Bank in McAllen via various routes to Green Mountain Holdings. This was a small fraction of the money the Gulf Cartel was making, but it was all the investigators could trace.

Ostensibly, Green Mountain also belonged to Aguirre and his family, but it was clear to investigators – and later to a jury – that it actually belonged to García Ábrego.

The sums being laundered were so large that they could not all be passed through First City Bank in Houston. Accounts in Harlingen National Bank and the International Bank of Commerce in Laredo, under the control of Luis Esteban García Villalón, were also used.

Suitcases full of small denomination bills arrived at the Texas Commerce Bank, courtesy of Mexico's former deputy attorney general Mario Ruiz Massieu. A judge ruled that this was drugs money belonging to García Ábrego and others.

But little of the laundered money could be traced. Brownsville alone is full of banks doing business with Mexican nationals. Even the San Antonio branch of the Federal Reserve bank found itself with an unexplained surplus in 1996. However, when the Internal Revenue Service investigated, they were unable to trace where $1 billion had come from. It was estimated that $30 billion of drugs money has entered the Texas banking system. Though bankers scrupulously obey the letter of the law, it is not in their interests to delve too deeply.

The money did not just go to crooked politicians and policemen. In Matamoros, people associated with García Ábrego owned farm machinery and auto dealerships, clothing and shoe stores, real estate and construction companies, hotels, restaurants, seed companies, gas stations and farms.

The Downfall of García Ábrego

As the sheer scale of García Ábrego's operation became clear, he began to keep a low profile and moved constantly from ranch to ranch and house to house. Then when Coello Trejo found that he had been short-changed, he turned up the heat and García Ábrego was forced underground.

In 1993, a Houston grand jury had already returned a thirty-two page indictment naming García Ábrego as 'the principal leader of a criminal enterprise headquartered in Matamoros which imported, warehoused, transported and distributed ton quantities of cocaine and marijuana'.

Then in 1995 he became the first drug trafficker to appear on the FBI's 'Most Wanted' list with a $2 million bounty on his head. However, the picture on the elusive García Ábrego's wanted poster was ten years out of date. But when the level of corruption in the Mexican government became apparent, police *comandantes* who for years had denied any knowledge of García Ábrego's whereabouts suddenly found they could track him down.

On 14 January 1996, policemen in riot gear hid in the shrubbery surrounding a red-tiled adobe hacienda outside Monterrey. When García Ábrego pulled into the driveway,

Portrait of a Cocaine King

One night in August 1993, the United States authorities in Brownsville, Texas, got a rare chance to get a glimpse of García Ábrego's personal life. His cousin Francisco Pérez Monroy, who had grown up with García Ábrego and was godfather to one of his children, sought to make a deal. Wanted on charges that could land him in jail, he waived his right to a lawyer, the authorities said, and with a tape recorder running painted a detailed picture of one of the most feared cartel leaders.

García Ábrego, he said, was a family man. He was superstitious and would grow violent if you tried to take his photograph. He drank tequila and Carta Blanca beer, and liked watching baseball, a game he had played as a boy. Hiding out in one of his many homes, he wore a Yankees cap, V-necked T-shirts, Sansabelt pants, boxer shorts and boots with zippers. Only his diamond-encrusted Rolex revealed that he was one of the world's richest men. That and a ring with a circle of diamonds on it and a gold chain around his neck sporting a cross and images of the saints.

Nevertheless, he spent as much as $80,000 a time on shopping sprees in the fashionable Joe Brand store in McAllen when buying clothes for Mexican officials, their families and their secretaries. Famously short-tempered, he shot an air-conditioning man dead when he had trouble fitting a new unit. He also had the ex-boyfriend of one of his sisters killed when he continued to telephone the family home, and ordered the murder of his mistress's former lover when he kept pestering her. These hits were traditionally ordered on the seventeenth of the month, to commemorate his brother Pepe who had died in an auto accident on 17 July 1982. And he always kept a pistol to hand, usually in the briefcase he carried.

He travelled with an entourage of bodyguards and used secret codes for mobile phone numbers that were changed constantly. Odd numbers were doubled, while even numbers were not. But he preferred to talk face to face and grew suspicious of anyone who was not where they were supposed to be.

As part of his entourage, he had a travelling witch-doctor and was rumoured to be part of a devil-worship cult who had sacrificed a student from the University of Texas on a ranch near Matamoros.

The constant stress of paying off politicians and policemen and making sure shipments arrived on time left him addicted to tranquillizers and unable to sleep. He came from a family with a history of heart trouble and had intermediaries keep an eye on his mother when she was in hospital in Brownsville and Houston. And he lived constantly in fear. In 1989 it was reported that he fled to Chicago for a year when an official in the attorney general's office found he had been short-changed in a bribe.

According to Pérez, García Ábrego was also trying to negotiate a surrender with the government of President Ernesto Zedillo. He would turn himself in, he said, provided that his relatives and girlfriends could keep their wealth and he would not be extradited to the United States where he could face the death penalty. He also wanted medical care for his jailed brother Humberto's diabetes.

He would also answer all questions put to him, he said, if he was allowed to take a farewell trip to Colombia, be arrested by the police officer of his choice, be incarcerated in Guadalajara with a number of his lieutenants for his protection, rather than in a maximum security prison with other cartel bosses, and be allowed conjugal visits from his mistresses. The government refused.

Pérez estimated that García Ábrego was worth $500 million. Suitcases full of money came in, sometimes still sprinkled with cocaine. There was

Acapulco is Mexico's playground of the rich. Ábrego is thought to have owned several nightclubs and hotels in the city

so much of it that bill-counting machines ran all night. Around $2 million was carted around Monterrey one night in plastic bags as if it were laundry. And he helped pay the bills of family, friends and associates.

He once gift-wrapped $50,000 and gave it to FBI agent Claude De la O – as a Christmas present, not a bribe, he said. García Ábrego was later charged with trying to bribe De la O, who was posing as a bent cop, with $100,000.

Along with his mansions and swimming pools, he also owned a string of legitimate businesses, including a trucking firm, a steelworks and a meat-packing plant in Monterrey. There were ranches where he kept his racehorses. His favourite was named *El Tejano* – 'The Texan'.

Pérez also identified photographs and picked out his cousin's ranches and home on maps. After testifying against García Ábrego in Houston, the heavily guarded Pérez and his family disappeared into the United States government's witness protection programme.

Ábrego's home outside Monterrey and the site of his arrest: he was overpowered, shot full of Valium and put on a plane to Houston

The Friend Killer

After the final fall of García Ábrego, Jesus Cruz Medrano, an editor at *El Bravo* wrote: 'The history of Matamoros during the reign of Juan García Ábrego was painted in blood and shame. For years, we have all lived in enormous fear.'

But the fear continued. With García Ábrego out of the way, there was a struggle for power inside the Gulf Cartel. His brother Humberto García Ábrego tried to take over, but his name alone made him a liability. Óscar Malherbe and his partner Raúl Valladares del Ángel replaced him briefly before they too were arrested.

Next came Hugo Baldomero Medina Garza – known as *El Señor de los Tráilers* ('Lord of the Trailers') for using trucks to traffic 20 tons of cocaine into the United States each month. Warned that ex-Marine Rafael Olvera López, aka *El Raffles*, was mounting a leadership challenge Medina Garza invited him to his office and pulled a gun on him. Before Olvera López could pull his own gun ex-cop turned trafficker Ángel Salvador 'El Chava' Gómez Herrera shot him in the back of the head, while Medina Garza fired from the front.

The following year, Gómez Herrera shot Medina Garza in the face, who survived. Gómez Herrera appointed Osiel Cárdenas Guillén in his place and when he recovered Medina Garza operated independently outside the cartel until he was captured and jailed in 2000. Meanwhile Cárdenas Guillén shot and killed Gómáz Herrera, earning him the nickname *El Mata Amigos* – 'The Friend Killer'.

he was overpowered, shot full of Valium and put on a plane to Houston. Even this was not an undiluted victory for the forces of law and order. It was alleged that the arresting officer, a *comandante* in the Federal Judicial Police, had been given $500,000 and a bullet-proof Mercury Grand Marquis by another cartel to secure his arrest.

This whirlwind extradition was also dubious. Mexico had passed laws – possibly thanks to politicians who took campaign funds from the cartels – forbidding the extradition of Mexican nationals, except in exceptional circumstances. However, when García Ábrego was 21, he had somehow obtained a United States birth certificate giving his birthplace as Las Paloma, Texas, possibly with the idea of emigrating there. This was enough to allow the Mexican government to deport him as an American citizen and an 'undesirable' alien. The day after García Ábrego's expulsion, the headline in *PM*, Matamoros's afternoon newspaper, read: 'An End to 10 Years of Narco Terror!'

Eight months after his arrest, García Ábrego was convicted of twenty-two counts of money laundering, drug possession and operating a criminal enterprise that prosecutors say smuggled more than 220,000 lbs (99,790 kg) of cocaine and 46,000 lbs (20,865 kg) of marijuana from Mexico into the United States over sixteen years. The jury found him guilty on all charges after being out for just twelve hours. He was sentenced to eleven consecutive life terms. The United States government had also requested that he hand over $1.05 billion, but the jury only awarded $350 million.

Osiel Cárdenas Guillén during his extradition from Mexico to the US in 2007

Confrontation in Matamoros

One afternoon in November 1989, a journalist who had been investigating the Gulf Cartel was being driven around Matamoros by FBI agent Daniel Fuentes and the DEA's Joe DuBois in a Ford Bronco with diplomatic plates. He was showing them the cartel's drug routes. They even drove past Cárdenas Guillén's pink stucco villa, which was surrounded by a high wall, security cameras, armed guards and roof-top snipers. Then they began to be followed, first by a Lincoln Continental and then by a stolen pick-up with Texas plates.

Just yards away from police headquarters, they were corralled by a convoy of armed gunmen, some wearing police and military uniforms. One of the gunmen, who appeared 'coked out of his head', was screaming 'Kill them!' Seconds later Cárdenas Guillén arrived in a Cherokee Jeep. He had a Colt pistol with a gold grip in his waistband and was carrying a gold-plated AK-47. The agents were asked to hand over their informant. Despite the overwhelming odds, they refused to do so.

'I knew what they'd do to me. I'd seen many pictures of the bodies they leave behind,' said DuBois. 'Dan and I decided, if we are going to die, we are going to die here.'

He explained that they were federal agents. Cárdenas Guillén said he did not give a damn who they were. DuBois replied: 'You don't care now, but tomorrow and the next day and the rest of your life, you'll regret anything stupid that you might do right now. You are fixing to make 300,000 enemies. Think it over, man. There is no way that you will be able to hide anywhere. They are going to come get you.'

All the time, in DuBois' mind, was the memory of what Kiki Camarena had endured before he died. And he had a Plan B. DuBois had a hidden gun strapped to his thigh. Fuentes had a gun in his hand.

'Unless they got Danny in a head shot, Osiel was coming with us,' said DuBois.

Outnumbered and outgunned, there was little chance they would survive.

'These guys were the most bloodthirsty killers in the Western Hemisphere,' he said. 'I was positive I wasn't going to make it. The immorality of killing someone doesn't go through their heads.'

Cárdenas Guillén's cohorts raised their guns, waiting for the order to fire. But Cárdenas faltered.

'You ******* gringos. This is my town, so get the **** out of here before I kill all of you,' he said. 'Don't return to my territory, you sons of whores, because you will die.'

DuBois and Fuentes were honoured for their exceptional bravery. Their informant was moved to the United States under the witness protection programme.

Fuentes said: 'This is probably the first time anybody had said "No" to Osiel and lived to talk about it.'

To secure his position, Cárdenas recruited thirty men from the Mexican Special Forces Airmobile Group (GAFE) as enforcers. They became *Los Zetas*. Cárdenas Guillén also featured on the FBI's 'Ten Most Wanted' list with a $2 million bounty on his head.

He was arrested after a shoot out with the Mexican military – some of whom were loyal GAFE troops – in Matamoros in 2003. But he continued to run the Gulf Cartel from prison, even organizing a children's party in the border town of Ciudád Acuña in Coahuila.

Cárdenas Guillén was later extradited to Texas where he was convicted of racketeering, homicide, drug trafficking, money laundering and threatening United States federal agents. He was sentenced to twenty-five years in jail and was forced to surrender $30 million.

In his absence, his lieutenants fought over the drug corridors. But the ultimate winners were *Los Zetas*, who went on to form a cartel of their own.

A soldier escorts Jesus Ivan Quezada, 'El Loco', an alleged member of Los Zetas. Quezada was a suspect in the murder of ICE agent Jaime Zapata whose car was attacked travelling along a highway in Mexico's San Luis Potosi state

LOS ZETAS

In 1997, the Mexican attorney general's office deployed the army in the northern states to combat drug trafficking. In charge of the operation was Mexico's drug czar, General José de Jesús Gutiérrez Rebollo, head of the *Instituto Nacional para el Combate a las Drogas*. However, a wiretap caught him accepting a bribe from Amado Carrillo Fuentes, head of the Juárez Cartel, and he was sentenced to over seventy years in jail with further charges outstanding. Cárdenas Guillén seized the opportunity to recruit Lieutenant Arturo Guzmán Decena, an officer in the Airborne Special Forces Group or GAFE who was serving in Tamaulipas.

Guzmán Decena brought with him another thirty or so deserters, who were offered salaries considerably higher than those paid by the Mexican government. Like all good gangsters they needed sobriquets. These included 'El Winnie Pooh', 'The Little Mother' and '*El Guerra*'.

Cárdenas Guillén expanded their role to collecting debts, securing cocaine supply and trafficking routes, discouraging defections from the cartel and executing its foes – often with unspeakable savagery. They took their name, *Los Zetas* – 'The Zs' – from the radio call sign of the GAFE. Guzmán Decena was Z-1.

In his struggle to take over the Gulf Cartel, Osiel Cárdenas Guillén then ordered Guzmán Decena (see page 40) to execute his partner, Salvador Gómez Herrera. The opportunity presented itself at the baptism of Cárdenas Guillén's daughter, where Gómez Herrera was to be a godfather. After the ceremony Cárdenas Guillén offered Gómez Herrera a ride in his Dodge Durango. Guzmán Decena was in the back seat. As the two men in the front laughed and joked, Guzmán Decena put a bullet in the back of *El Chava*'s head, splattering his brains across the leather dashboard. His corpse, partially eaten by scavengers, was found in the brush outside Matamoros some time later.

After Guzmán Decena had been killed by the authorities in 2002, his second-in-command Rogelio '*El Kelín*' González Pizaña took over. González was arrested in October 2004 at a party in La Covacha, a brothel owned by the Zetas in Matamoros. He tried to escape in his armoured Volkswagen Passat, throwing grenades at agents and soldiers in his path, but he was shot through the left side of the chest in the firefight. One federal agent died, along with two suspected members of González's gang, one of whom burned to death in the Volkswagen Passat, which became engulfed in flames during the gun battle. Twenty-two table dancers also spent a night in the slammer.

El Kelín was replaced by Heriberto Lazcano Lazcano, aka *El Verdugo* – 'The Executioner'. Like Guzmán he was ex-Special Forces. With Osiel Cárdenas Guillén in jail, Lazcano and his principal henchman Jaime 'The Hummer' González Durán felt they owed no particular allegiance to Cárdenas Guillén's brother Antonio Ezequiel – aka *Tony Tormenta* ('Tony the Storm') – and his partner, former municipal police officer Jorge Eduardo Costilla Sánchez.

Drug czar General José de Jesús Gutiérrez Rebollo was caught accepting a bribe and sentenced to seventy years in jail

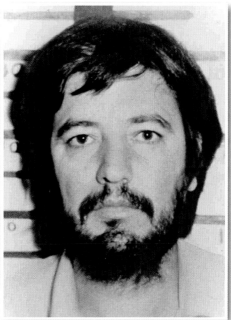

Amado Carrillo Fuentes was head of the Juárez Cartel. He seized control after assassinating Rafael Aguilar Guajardo

Osiel Cárdenas Guillén offered Gómez Herrera a ride in his Dodge Durango, which proved to be a one-way ticket to hell

ABOVE *The Mexican Army Special Forces proved to be the ideal recruiting ground for new members of the drug cartels*

LEFT *Heriberto 'The Executioner' Lazcano was ex-Special Forces. He was infamous for his merciless brutality*

Unleashing a Lion

Some of *Los Zetas* thought Lazcano should head the Gulf Cartel. Rather than take them on, *Los Zetas* began drug running on their own account and earned 'black money' from gambling dens, massage parlours, table-dancing clubs, brothels and nightclubs. They also siphoned oil from Mexico's pipelines.

'The Gulf Cartel created the lion, but now the lion has wised up and controls the handler,' said a United States law enforcement officer. 'The Zetas don't ask the Gulf Cartel permission for anything any more. They simply inform them of their activities whenever they feel like it.'

Camps were set up to train raw young recruits aged fifteen to eighteen, as well as ex-police officers. These were also joined by men from Guatemala's counter-insurgency Special Forces, known as the Kaibiles. Their motto was: 'If I advance, follow me. If I stop, urge me on. If I retreat, kill me.'

Los Zetas were armed with AR-15 and AK-47 assault rifles, MP5 sub-machine guns, 50 mm machine guns, grenade launchers, ground-to-air missiles, dynamite, bazookas and helicopters – many of the weapons provided by veterans of the Gulf War. Like Special Forces troops, they wore dark clothing and sometimes blackened their faces. They also drove brand-new SUVs, usually stolen, and carried the image of the narco-saint Jesús Malverde. And they were known for their merciless brutality. Lazcano, for example, delighted in lowering victims – men, women and children – into vats of boiling oil. In Nuevo Laredo, four police officers were put inside barrels filled with diesel fuel and set on fire.

Los Zetas *went to great lengths to recover the bodies of fallen comrades. In 2007, four armed men broke into the graveyard in Poza Rica, smashed open a tomb and made off with the body of Roberto Carlos Carmona*

Lazcano also gunned down Francisco Ortiz Franco, editor of a crusading newspaper in Tijuana, in front of his children. Under his leadership, the severed heads of two policemen in Acapulco were found on spikes outside a government building with a message signed 'Z' that read: 'So that you learn respect.' Lazcano himself was said to favour starving captured rivals to death. At other times he allowed them to be eaten by the wild animals he imported from Africa for hunting practice. He also liked racehorses, fast cars and blonde women. Mexico put a $2.6 million bounty on his head; the United States added another $5 million.

Despite their excesses, *Los Zetas* maintained their *esprit de corps*, often going to great lengths to recover the body of a fallen comrade. In 2007, four armed men broke into the graveyard in the town of Poza Rica, Veracruz, tied up a security guard, smashed open a tomb and made off with the ornate coffin containing Roberto Carlos Carmona, who had been shot to death in a fight over a horse race.

Arturo Guzmán Decena

Born in 1976 in a small village in Puebla, southern Mexico, Arturo Guzmán Decena joined the army to escape poverty. He went on to join the elite GAFE, Mexico's equivalent of the Green Berets or the SAS. The unit's motto was: 'Not even death will stop us, and if it surprises us, then it is welcome.'

He trained with the Israeli Defense Forces, at the infamous School of the Americas (SOA) in Georgia and Fort Bragg in North Carolina, home to the United States Army's Special Forces. When the Latin American students' training manuals were declassified in 1996, they caused controversy. One called *Handling of Sources* instructed them how to get the best out of informants, or 'employees': 'The Counter Insurgency agent could cause the arrest of the employee's parents, imprison the employee or give him a beating as part of the placement plan of the said employee in the guerilla organization.'

Back in Mexico, Guzmán Decena and the GAFE used what they had been taught to suppress the Zapatistas, largely indigenous Mayans protesting about poverty and one-party rule. Armed only with old shotguns and .22 rifles, they had already fled from the regular army units when Guzmán Decena's unit caught up with them at the town of Ocosingo on the edge of the jungle. Within hours, thirty-four rebels were dead. The Zapatista leadership insisted that although these men had surrendered they had been summarily executed. The next day, three more rebels were captured. Their corpses were found on a riverbank with their ears and noses cut off.

Sent north to the border, Guzmán Decena discovered the garish mansions of the wealthy narco bosses, all-night parties and flocks of young prostitutes. It was a change from the mud of the jungle. Like other soldiers, Guzmán Decena took bribes from Cárdenas Guillén to turn a blind eye to drug trafficking. However, as Mexico moved towards a more open democracy, the families of the 'disappeared' marched daily in the capital and army officers began to find themselves on trial. It was then that Guzmán Decena went to work for Cárdenas Guillén, taking other military personnel with him.

Following the murder of Gómez Herrera, Cárdenas Guillén took sole charge of the Gulf Cartel. With the support of Guzmán Decena and *Los Zetas* there was no opposition, but his reign did not last long. Guzmán Decena was killed on 22 November 2002.

According to the campaigning news magazine ironically called *Zeta*, Guzmán Decena had a drink and a couple of lines of cocaine and then decided to visit his mistress, Ana Bertha González Lagunes. As usual, he got his henchmen to close off the street where she lived, so the traffic noise would not disturb their lovemaking. The neighbours were fed up with this and called the police. Normally nothing happened, but this time a neighbour contacted the *Unidad Especial contra la Delincuencia Organizada* (UEDO) – the 'Special Anti-Organized Crime Unit'. They called for support from the army. In the ensuing gunfight, three of Guzmán Decena's men were killed and another was injured. Guzmán Decena was very drugged, could not defend himself and was shot down.

Floral tributes were left on the sidewalk where he had fallen. One was accompanied by a note that read: 'You will always be in our hearts. From your family, *Los Zetas*.'

There were unsubstantiated reports that Guzmán Decena had been killed on the orders of 'The Friend Killer', who was scared of his growing power.

By 2008, there were between one hundred and two hundred *Los Zetas*. Alongside them were other formations. *Los Halcones* – 'The Hawks' – watched over the *plazas*. There were eighty of them, equipped with powerful radio transmitters, in Matamoros alone. *Las Ventanas* – 'The Windows' – were teenagers on bikes employed to look out for the police and other people taking an interest in the activities of the drug dealers. *Dirección* – 'Command' – comprised some twenty communications experts, who tapped phones, identified suspicious automobiles and set up kidnappings and assassinations. Then there were *Las Leopardas* – 'The Leopards' – prostitutes who milked information from their clients.

Under Lazcano, *Los Zetas* became more independent. They forged links with *La Familia* enforcer gangs in Michoacán, a centre for cocaine trafficking and methamphetamine laboratories, where they regularly crossed swords with the Sinaloa Cartel.

Cartels United

Fearing the rise of *Los Zetas*, the Gulf Cartel joined forces with the Sinaloa Cartel and *La Familia* – who switched sides – calling themselves the *Carteles Unidos* – 'Cartels United'. In a video on YouTube, they said:

> *'Without the "Z" you will live without fear… If you are a Zeta, run because the monster is coming… the new alliance has raised its weapons to f• • • the Zetas because they have undermined the drug trafficking business with their kidnappings, extortions, etc. To sum it up, they don't give a sh•t about the freedom and tranquillity of the Mexican people.'*

In Matamoros, the Gulf Cartel hung up banners, known as *narcomantas*, in the street, saying: 'The Gulf Cartel distances itself from the Z. In our ranks we do not want

Jaime 'The Hummer' González Durán is paraded by his captors in Mexico City, in 2008, before being sentenced to seventy-three years in jail. Before he joined Los Zetas, *he had been in the Mexican Air Force*

kidnappers, terrorists, bank-robbers, rapists, child-killers and traitors.'

Others elsewhere in the state said: 'People of Tamaulipas, don't be afraid. We are only looking out for your wellbeing.' Or: 'We are trained individuals, not children. We respect women. We don't kill civilians. We are from Tamaulipas and we respect our own.'

Clearly a war was beginning. People were warned to stay indoors at night and to report any Zetas to the Gulf Cartel.

The Zetas responded with their own banners and leaflets, saying that they had only carried out kidnappings and executions on the Gulf Cartel's orders; they were their enforcers. They also said that the Gulf Cartel had killed civilians and set fire to their homes so they could blame the atrocities on the Zetas.

The *Carteles Unidos* struck back with banners distancing themselves from attacks on a federal building and calling on President Felipe de Jesús Calderón Hinojosa to join them in eradicating the Zetas.

At first the *Carteles Unidos*'s *mantas* had an effect on public opinion, but soon they seemed like banners outside a supermarket offering two for one. This coincided with the diminution of any respect the public had for the cartels. Earlier they had seemed to have a code of conduct, going about their business away from the public view and basically only killing their own. Now they seemed to be filled with drugged-up kids wielding machine guns.

The Zetas also used their banners to recruit those still in the military. In the army, the diet consisted largely of packets of dried noodles. *Los Zetas* promised that if recruits joined them they would not have to eat them any more. And soon more Special Operations troops defected.

Los Zetas also made alliances with the Juárez Cartel, the Tijuana Cartel and the Beltrán-Leyva Cartel. However, there was talk of a rivalry inside the Zetas between Lazcano and Miguel Ángel Treviño Morales, who had risen to prominence after 'The Hummer' was arrested in the northern city of Reynosa in 2008. He was found to be in possession of 540 rifles, 165 grenades, 500,000 rounds of ammunition and 14 sticks of TNT. At his trial he was sentenced to thirty-five years for kidnapping and organized crime, twenty-one years for weapons possession and sixteen-and-a-half years for money laundering.

Miguel Ángel Treviño Morales

Treviño Morales – Z-40, or *El 40* – was not a member of the original Zetas, or *Zetas Viejos* as they were now called, though he sometimes claimed to be a former member of the GAFE. Born in 1973 in Nuevo Laredo, he worked for García Ábrego before becoming a policeman in Reynosa. He spoke fluent English and became an expert in running contraband across the border. But after several brushes with the Dallas County Sheriff's Department and the Federal District Court of North Texas, in 2008, the Federal District Court for the District of Columbia issued a warrant for his arrest. The following year, he was indicted in New York for 'numerous acts of violence, including murder, kidnappings, tortures, and collection of drug debts'.

Treviño Morales had a reputation for savagery: his favourite way of killing people was to put his victims in an oil drum, douse them in gasoline and burn them alive

A refrigerated truck containing seventy bodies exhumed from a mass grave found in San Fernando, Tamaulipas arrives at the Forensic Medical Service, Mexico City, 2011. Morales was thought to have been responsible

He already had a reputation for savagery. In 2005, he directed the battle against the Sinaloa Cartel for the control of Nuevo Laredo. At his behest, the local police arrested thirty-four of his foes and took them to a house in the city's Benito Juárez neighbourhood. Treviño Morales then arrived in a black Special Forces uniform. He ordered 17-year-old Felipe López – aka *El Güerillo* – to be separated from the others. When he resisted, Treviño Morales' henchman *El Maco* bound his wrists.

'Which of you knows where the heart is?' asked Treviño Morales, as he plunged a knife into his victim's chest. Felipe López died immediately.

Next he turned to a hostage named *El Ruco* – 'The Old One' – and asked him how old he was. He replied: 'Fifty-two'.

'You have lived too long,' said Treviño Morales. 'You are going to join the *muchacho*.'

The two bodies were shoved into the boot of a compact car to be disposed of. However, it was reported that Treviño Morales' favourite way of killing people was the *guiso* – 'stew'. They were put in an oil drum, doused with gasoline and burned alive. He also liked dismembering people while they were still living. The dumping of dismembered bodies became his calling card.

Treviño Morales developed the status of a cult figure in the Mexican underworld. He was said to have escaped unscathed from several gun battles, he refused to make deals and he seemed unafraid to die. This established his position as Lazcano's number two.

In February 2008, Treviño Morales was sent to Guatemala to take control of the drug-smuggling routes there. He was thought to have fired the bullet that took out the Guatemalan drug boss Juan José 'Juancho' Leon.

The bodies of seventy-two undocumented immigrants, mainly from Central America, were found in a mass grave in August 2010. They had been reportedly murdered by the Zetas. The Zetas had intercepted several buses heading towards two border towns and had kidnapped those on board. Another 193 people were killed on a ranch near San Fernando in April 2011. Treviño Morales was thought to be responsible for both atrocities.

The finger was pointed at him again in May 2012, when the bodies of forty-nine people – minus their heads, hands and feet – were dumped around a busy highway in northern Mexico.

Ramiro Villarreal – *El Gordo* or 'Fatso' – became an informant for the DEA to avoid being prosecuted himself. He was an associate of Treviño Morales' brother José, who ran a racehorse business north of the border – clearly a way to launder money. Ramiro Villarreal was barely making a living because the Treviño Morales brothers extorted horses out of him and trimmed his travelling expenses.

Then Villarreal was called to a meeting with *Papi* ('Daddy'), meaning Z-40 himself. He was blindfolded, then taken out into the Mexican desert, where he saw two vats which were normally used to make *pozole*, the name of a local stew. But in this case they were filled with acid. People were cut up and then dropped in – within a short time only their teeth remained.

'Where's *Papi*?' Villarreal asked nervously.

When Treviño Morales turned up, he hugged Villarreal and asked: 'You're not screwing me, are you, *Gordo*?'

'Of course not, *Papi*,' said Villarreal.

Saying he would be back in a minute, Treviño Morales walked over to another man, shot him in the head and had his body dropped into one of the vats of acid.

Villarreal passed out. When he awoke Treviño Morales was slapping him in the face and laughing.

'What's wrong, *Gordo*?' he said. 'You can't handle seeing me kill someone? Next time, I'm going to have you do it.'

'No, *Papi*,' said Villarreal. 'I don't want there to be a next time.'

There wasn't. Next time he was seen by the authorities, he was barely able to walk because of gangrene in one leg. Then his charred remains were found in a burned-out car outside Nuevo Laredo. Only DNA samples identified the body.

By all accounts Treviño Morales was a psychopath who could not sleep at night unless he had killed someone. Stories also circulated that he liked eating the hearts of his victims, believing that it would make him invincible.

As a youth he had criss-crossed the border with his mother, after they had been abandoned by his father. Having spent much of his youth in Dallas, he bore a grudge about the way Mexican immigrants were treated. In October 2010, after his mother had been harassed by United States Customs in Laredo, he ordered grenades to be tossed at the United States Consulate in Monterrey. The following year, two United States immigration officers were shot as they drove along a major highway in Central Mexico at midday.

'He always had a chip on his shoulder, which explains his explosive personality,' said a United States law enforcement official. 'He really believed that in Mexico you gain power, respect with brute force.'

He also surrounded himself with unthinking killers, recruiting young people who felt that they had been screwed by society. After placing a gun in the hand of one of the recruits he would pick a victim at random, put his hand over the initiate's heart to feel how fast it was beating and then say: '*Chíngatelo!*' – 'F**k him over!' If the trainee hesitated, Treviño Morales would take his gun and either put a bullet to his head or offer him a job as a lookout, depending on his mood on the day.

Children as young as twelve were recruited as assassins. They were called *Zetistas* and Treviño Morales would give a boy of fifteen a 100,000-dollar Mercedes if he thought he had earned it.

Having won the battle against the Sinaloa Cartel in Nuevo Laredo, Treviño Morales took over in Nuevo León and Piedras Negras, Coahuila. He went into people smuggling, pirating CDs and DVDs, kidnapping, extortion and intimidation. When Efraín Teodoro Torres – Z-14 – was killed in a gun battle over a horse race, Treviño Morales took over in Veracruz to the south of Tamaulipas.

He backed Lazcano in the split from the Gulf Cartel and was promoted to become national commander of *Los Zetas*, a position normally held by someone who had a military background. Treviño Morales proved his credentials by threatening to shoot down the plane of President Felipe Calderón, who was visiting Tamaulipas in August 2012.

Treviño Morales Takes Over

Carlos de Santiago [left], Iván Velázquez Caballero ('El Talibán') [centre] and Manuel Guerrero (aka 'Tony') are paraded before the cameras after being captured by the Mexican Navy in 2012

Treviño Morales was far from popular in *Los Zetas*. After Z-7 – Jesús Enrique Rejón Aguilar, aka *El Mamito* – had been captured, a '*narcocorrido*' music video was posted on YouTube. It accused him of betraying Rejón Aguilar and other Zetas to the authorities and of being a Judas who was disloyal to Lazcano. During the feud, Iván Velázquez Caballero – *El Talibán* – leader of the faction opposing Treviño Morales, was arrested by the Mexican Navy on 26 September 2012.

Salvador Alfonso Martinez Escobedo, aka *El Ardilla* – 'The Squirrel' – was captured on 6 October. He was wanted in connection with the massacre of the seventy-two immigrants found in Tamaulipas in 2010, the escape of 151 prisoners in Nuevo Laredo and 131 in Piedras Negras and

the killing of United States citizen David Hartley, who was sailing on Falcon Lake which straddles the border.

The following day Lazcano was killed in a shoot out with the navy in Progreso, Coahuila. The authorities found a grenade launcher, twelve grenades and two rifles in his vehicle. Fortunately, Lazcano's fingerprints had been taken, confirming the corpse was his, before it was snatched from the funeral home.

Treviño Morales now took over the Zetas, but a faction calling themselves *Los Legionarios* – 'The Legionaries' – split off. Banners announced:

'The Legionaries are a group of renegade Zetas who were betrayed by Z-40. The Legionaries have the clear mission only to kill people from the Zetas and their families... an eye for an eye. Our business is solely and exclusively drug trafficking. We respect the federal forces and their fight to end the narco.'

They were followed by another anti-Treviño Morales faction called *Sangre Zeta* – 'Zeta Blood'. Then came the *Golfo Nueva Generación* – 'Gulf New Generation' – in Matamoros and *Corona* – 'Crown' – made up of gangsters once loyal to the Sinaloa Cartel.

Treviño Morales took to sleeping in a vehicle with the engine running and always carried enough money to bribe his way out of any jam. He was also said to travel in low-flying aircraft or in an ambulance surrounded by a convoy of otherwise respectable citizens.

The battleground again was Nuevo Laredo. In 2012 some 550 bodies were recovered in the city, making the murder rate 143 per 100,000. This compared with 56 per 100,000 in Ciudad Juárez, the country's most notorious hotbed of crime.

Run to Ground

In June 2013, the authorities learned that Treviño Morales had fathered a baby. He doted on the child and was paying regular visits. On the night of 16 July 2013, he was travelling over the back roads of Tamaulipas when he found himself confronted by a Black Hawk helicopter. The pick-up pulled to a halt. Three men jumped out.

Two hit the ground. The third – Treviño Morales – made a run for it, but was taken by a ground force of Mexican marines without a shot being fired. Eight rifles and $2 million were found in the vehicle.

With Miguel Ángel Treviño Morales in a maximum security prison, the Zetas were taken over by his younger brother Óscar Omar Treviño Morales – Z-42. The United States authorities put a $5 million bounty on his head.

Two other brothers were already in jail in the United States and a nephew was incarcerated in Mexico. Another nephew had been killed in a shoot out.

Jesús Malverde, Narco-saint

Although not recognized by the Catholic Church, Jesús Malverde is a legendary bandit and the patron saint of drug traffickers. He is also known as the 'Generous One' and the 'Angel of the Poor' because of his supposed support for the downtrodden in the struggle against dictatorship. His image, which is thought to offer protection from the law, is found on a range of items from T-shirts and cologne

to household cleaners and patches sewn on to jackets and backpacks. Busts of Malverde, looking suspiciously like Pedro Infante, a Mexican matinee idol of the 1940s, sit next to the cash registers in restaurants, bars and discotheques.

Mexico's answer to Robin Hood, Malverde was said to have been hanged in 1909. A shrine has been built over what is thought to be his grave in Culiacán, Sinaloa. It is regularly visited by drug traffickers who go to give thanks.

In 2003, a manufacturer in Los Angeles started making products featuring Jesús Malverde, which included candles, rosaries, trading cards, stamps, hair oils and bathroom cleaners. They even export them to Italy, joking that they are going to the Mafia.

The popularity of the narco-saint was a gift for the police. They look out for cars with Malverde symbols on the windshield or hanging from the rear-view mirror. Courts in California, Kansas, Nebraska and Texas have ruled that Malverde trinkets, talismans and tattoos are admissible evidence in drug and money laundering cases.

The Mexican brewer Cervcería Minerva began producing a beer called Malverde in 2008.

'Drug smugglers drink it like holy water,' said Sergeant Rico Garcia of the Houston Police Department.

A Mexican boy prays in the Malverde Chapel in Culiacán, Sinaloa. Malverde, aka 'the narco-saint', is the patron saint of drug smugglers

The coffin of the Tijuana police chief Alfredo de la Torre Marquez on the day of his funeral, 29 February 2000: he died in a hail of gunfire after his car was ambushed as he drove home from mass. The vehicle was riddled with over 100 bullets

THE TIJUANA CARTEL

When Miguel Ángel Félix Gallardo divided up the Guadalajara Cartel *plazas* at the Acapulco conference in 1987, he reserved the drug route through Tijuana for himself, with the help of the Arellano Félix brothers. His former lieutenants Héctor Luis Palma Salazar – '*El Guëro*' – and Joaquín '*El Chapo*' Guzmán continued to run the Pacific operation or Sinaloa Cartel.

The Arellano Félix clan's middle-class parents, Francisco Arellano Sánchez and Alicia Isabel Félix Azueta, had raised eleven children in Sinaloa. Five of them (Benjamín, Ramón, Francisco Rafael, Francisco Javier and Eduardo) began smuggling clothing and electronic goods before going into trafficking drugs.

Félix Gallardo was arrested in 1989, but he continued to keep his hand on the tiller from jail, via a mobile phone, until he was transferred to a new high security prison at Altiplano in 1991. The Sinaloa Cartel was then taken over by its leaders and the Arellano Félix brothers set up the Tijuana Cartel, or Arellano-Félix Organization (AFO).

Félix Gallardo had originally favoured Francisco Javier Caro Payán, but Payán had been arrested in Canada in 1987, on marijuana smuggling charges. His place was taken by Jesús Labra Avilés – aka '*El Chuy*', the diminutive of Jesús – the cartel's financial mastermind, with Benjamín Arellano Félix as chief strategist and Ramón Arellano Félix as enforcer. This caused a lingering enmity with Rafael Caro Quintero, who was Caro Payán's cousin.

Ramón was known for his innovative ways of killing people. He would suffocate people with clear plastic bags while his henchman *El Gordo* jumped up and down on their chests. Or he would give them a 'Colombian necktie'. This was reserved for informants. He would cut their throats under the chin and pull their tongues out through the wound.

ABOVE *Félix Gallardo had been arrested in 1989, but continued to run operations from jail via a mobile phone*

RIGHT *Benjamin [left] and Ramón Arellano Félix – two middle-class boys with a penchant for violent murder*

'Wherever there is danger, that's where you'll find Ramón,' a former 'narco-junior', Alejandro Hodoyán, told Mexican narcotics agents in 1996 in an interview later run by the Mexican magazine *Proceso*. 'In 1989 or '90, we were at a Tijuana corner without anything to do and he told us, "Let's go kill someone. Who has a score to settle?" Cars would pass and he'd ask us who we knew. The person we pointed out would appear dead within a week.'

The two leaders of the Sinaloa Cartel, Joaquín Guzmán and his business partner Héctor Luis Palma Salazar, attempted to take control of Tijuana from the Arellano-Félix Organization in the late 1980s. In 1989, after a number of violent incidents, *El Chapo* Guzmán sent his trusted lieutenant Armando López, aka *El Rayo* – 'The Ray'– to speak with the Arellano Félixes in Tijuana. Before López had a chance to meet them face to face, he was killed by Ramón. The Tijuana Cartel then ordered a hit on the remaining López family members to prevent reprisals. Tit-for-tat killings ensued until eight members of the Tijuana Cartel were gunned down in a discotheque in Puerto Vallarta, Jalisco. However, the principal targets, Ramón and Francisco Javier, escaped unscathed and were eager for revenge.

A hit squad was sent to Guadalajara International Airport to take out *El Chapo*. When they spotted a white Mercury Grand Marquis, a car favoured by narcos, they opened fire. But it was not carrying Guzmán, who was sitting in a dark green Buick sedan nearby. He escaped the scene by taxi. The Grand Marquis was carrying Cardinal Juan Jesús Posadas Ocampo, whose body was struck by fourteen bullets. He was killed along with six bystanders.

Seven months later Francisco Rafael Arellano Félix was arrested for drug trafficking, firearms offences and complicity in the murder of Cardinal Posadas Ocampo. He was sentenced to ten years. However, in 1980 he had been arrested in California for selling nine ounces of cocaine to an undercover federal agent and had jumped bail. So after his sentence in Mexico was completed he was extradited to the United States, where he faced another six years in jail.

The other kingpins in the Tijuana Cartel were Ismael 'El Mayel' Higuera Guerrero, money launderer and boss in Ensenada, forty miles (65 km) down the coast from Tijuana, and Arturo Everardo 'El Kitty' Páez Martínez, who specialized in recruiting the violent offspring of the good families in Tijuana. They were used as torturers and assassins to discourage other traffickers from using

the Mexicali–Tijuana corridor without paying the transit tax demanded by the Arellano-Félix Organization (AFO). The AFO spread its tentacles across the border into San Diego and used foreign mercenaries to bolster its paramilitary structure.

Higuera Guerrero was arrested in 2000. Extradited to the United States in 2007, he was sent to the Supermax prison in Colorado and is due to be released in 2040. The following year, Arturo Páez became the first Mexican drug trafficker to be handed over. Sent to the United States in 2001, he was sentenced to thirty years for shipping cocaine.

El Chuy Labra Avilés was also arrested in 2000 while watching his son playing football. Accused of possessing an illegal firearm, he was placed under house arrest for three months. Drug trafficking and organized crime charges followed and he went to the maximum security prison at Almoloya de Juárez. A few days after his arrest, his lawyer, Gustavo Galvez Reyes, was found tortured and killed.

Ramón Arellano Félix was killed when he was in Mazatlán, Sinaloa, ostensibly to kill drug lord Ismael Zambada García. When he was stopped by a police officer for a minor traffic infraction, he pulled a gun and shot the cop. As the officer fell, he fired, killing Ramón. It was rumoured that the cop who shot him was in the pay of the Sinaloa Cartel. The identification card on Ramón's body read 'Jorge Pérez López' – the Mexican equivalent of John Doe. Only later, when photos from the crime scene were examined, did the authorities realize that one of the FBI's ten most wanted fugitives had been shot down. By then his body had disappeared from the funeral home.

A mobile phone found near the corpse had recently been used to make calls to Puebla, a small town 65 miles

(105 km) southeast of Mexico City. Added to that, a cartel money courier had been tracked to the same town and a girl with an unusually large chin had recently moved there with her family. Benjamín Arellano Félix's daughter was known to have a facial deformity. Locals knew the cigar-smoking drug lord as Manuel Treviño.

When the authorities burst into Benjamín's suburban home, they found candles burning at a shrine to Ramón and stacks of money littering the floor. He was arrested and extradited to California, where he was sentenced to twenty-five years for racketeering and money laundering

ABOVE *Higuera Guerrero was arrested in 2000 and extradited to a Supermax prison in Colorado*

RIGHT *Ramón Arellano Félix lies dead by the roadside alongside the police officer who flagged him down*

after a plea bargain saved him from a possible 140 years in jail. However, he faces another twenty-two years in jail when he is returned to Mexico at the end of his sentence in the United States.

Francisco Javier Arellano Félix, aka *El Tigrillo* – 'Little Tiger' – was fishing on his yacht, the *Doc Holliday*, when he was captured by the United States Coast Guard. He pleaded guilty to running a criminal enterprise and conspiring to launder money. Imposing a mandatory life sentence, United States District Judge Larry A. Burns said: 'Your family's name will live in infamy.'

Nevertheless the AFO was still very much a going concern. Soon after the arrest of *El Tigrillo*, the authorities uncovered a maze of tunnels connecting Tijuana with San Diego, some of which had concrete flooring and electric lights.

Eduardo Arellano Félix, aka *El Médico* because he had trained as a doctor, was left in charge. He was arrested in 2008 after a three-hour gun battle with Mexican soldiers and police at his home in a wealthy neighbourhood of Tijuana. Then he was extradited to the United States, where Judge Burns sentenced him to just fifteen years

The Stew-maker

Santiago Meza López was called *El Pozolero* – 'The Stew-maker' – after *pozole*, a Mexican meat soup.

Born in Guamúchil, Sinaloa in 1976, at the age of nineteen he went to work as a construction worker for the 'big guys' operating along the border. Then he joined the Arellano Félix family as a full-time operative. In 2000, the family decided to introduce a new method of disposing of their enemies. Until then, they had simply dumped their bodies in the sewers or the city's river. But this was risky and a corpse was a valuable piece of evidence.

The AFO brought in two 'teachers' from Israel, who taught a bunch of gang members how to dissolve corpses in acid. One of the cartel's pupils was Meza López. He used oil drums and caustic soda which he bought from a hardware store at $1.50 a pound. About a hundred pounds of powder was used to dissolve each corpse.

'A lady once asked me the reason why I bought so much caustic soda,' said Meza López. 'I told her I used it to clean houses.'

He was assisted by two 25-year-olds named *El Chalino* and *El Yiyo*, also from Guamúchil, who had come to Tijuana to make money. Meza López taught them to 'make *pozole*'.

It was a dangerous business. They had to wear latex gloves and gas masks.

'The corpses that I was given to make *pozole* were already dead,' he insisted. He did not cut them up, but dumped them complete inside the oil drums.

This was done on property alongside the road to Tecate, in a desolate area called Ojo de Agua.

'That's where the *pozole* was dumped,' he said. 'We dumped about sixty corpses there.'

They also used a small ranch in the outskirts of Tijuana, along Boulevard 2000.

'But my only task was to get rid of the bodies!' Meza López said. He even saw this as a normal job and was paid $600 a week, plus the ingredients for his meat soup.

He was working for the Tijuana Cartel when he met Teodoro García Simental and when *El Teo* split from Fernando Sánchez Arellano *El Pozolero* went with him and continued his duties.

'*El Teo* would call me and tell me that at a certain hour, in a certain place, I was to be given the merchandise,' said Meza López. 'They would call me and tell me in which car they were. They would make a light signal and the delivery was made.'

At the height of the fight between García Simental and the Arellano Félix Organization, he was disposing of over thirty bodies a month.

In January 2009, he was seized when the army

Santiago Meza López confessed to dissolving the bodies of 300 victims – at one point he was disposing of over thirty bodies a month

made a raid on a party in the Baja Seasons Hotel in Ensenada. He was cooking – this time sea food – and was too drunk to run away.

Driven back to Tijuana in a Humvee, he was heard repeatedly saying 'sorry, sorry' and asking God for his forgiveness. The police had been expecting a dangerous hit man. Instead the army brought them a short man with a well-trimmed moustache who walked with a lumbering gait and had difficulty breathing and moving.

He admitted disposing of over three hundred corpses, but as he had done his work so effectively they could not be found or identified, so no charges could be brought. Instead he was sent to El Rincon Federal Prison in Nayarit for the possession of illegal firearms.

Four years later, Meza López made a tearful appearance at a press conference, begging to be released. He told the journalists that he did not know the identities of the corpses he had disposed of, but had simply been doing his job.

Fernando Ocegueda Flores, president of the *Asociacion Unidos por los Desaparecidos* – United Association for the Disappeared – opposed Santiago Meza López's release. He said that the relatives 'won't forgive Santiago. They don't believe in his tears. He's an evil being, even though Santiago didn't kill their relatives, they believe that only someone mentally disturbed would desecrate a corpse like that. We believe that he asked for forgiveness because he was still drugged and felt his whole world falling apart'.

When they asked him for help, he would tell them where the remains of the relatives were buried.

'He shouldn't be free, he must be in jail. The only thing he knows is to make *pozole*, and he'll go back to his old habits,' said Fernando Ocegueda.

because he was 'less involved in the unsavoury aspects of the drug business'. However, he was an integral part of the cartel and was fully aware of its methods. He also faces further imprisonment when he is returned to Mexico at the end of his sentence.

This left sister Enedina Arellano Félix, an accountant, as titular head of the cartel, in partnership with her son Luis Fernando Sánchez Arellano, aka *El Ingeniero* – 'The Engineer'. The organization was further weakened by the arrest of Gustavo Rivera Martínez – *El EP1* – in a raid on one of the Tijuana Cartel's safe houses. One of the largest arsenals of weapons ever found in Mexico was discovered, including guns encrusted with gold figures and skulls.

The depleted organization had lost its Colombian contacts. As the supply of cocaine dried up, it relied more on the trafficking of marijuana and methamphetamines. It also diversified into kidnapping, auto theft, extortion, murder for hire and people trafficking.

El Teo

One of the Tijuana Cartel's *pistoleros*, Teodoro García Simental – *El Teo* or *El Tres Letras* for the three letters in 'Teo' – fell out with Fernando Arellano after the arrest of his brother 'El Chris'. The war between the two factions stepped up in November 2008 with the murder of *El Teo*'s 25-year-old girlfriend Karla Priscila Carrasco Agüero, aka *La Del Telcel* – 'The Cellphone Girl'.

After a shoot out on an expressway in eastern Tijuana, which left fourteen dead, García Simental fled to Sinaloa, but returned to launch an all-out war with the backing of Joaquín 'El Chapo' Guzmán and Ismael 'El Mayo' Zambada García, leaders of the Sinaloa Cartel.

Tijuana was soon averaging five killings per day. Many of the bodies carried messages boasting that they were the work of García Simental. One victim was found with his face sliced off. It had been sewn on to a soccer ball with a note to the police saying: 'Happy New Year, because this will be your last.'

The victim was 26-year-old Hugo Hernandez, who had been kidnapped. His body was cut up into seven pieces. The torso was found in a plastic container in a separate location from a box containing his arms, legs and head – all some distance from the macabre soccer ball.

Three headless bodies were dumped near a baseball

LEFT *Teodoro García Simental ('El Teo') had such a fearsome reputation that the authorities were too scared to include his photograph on their wanted posters in case he retaliated*

RIGHT *Eleven alleged members of the Sinaloa Cartel are brought to book after being captured in La Paz city, Baja California*

beheading victims… This generation is setting a new standard for savagery.'

This was celebrated in *narcocorrido* ballads. One song boasted: 'Pay attention President… In Tijuana, I rule. We'll show you what a real war is like.'

One of *El Teo*'s lieutenants, Raydel López Uriarte was known as *El Muletas* – 'The Crutches' – for the trail of disabled people he left behind him. He fitted out his crews in fake uniforms, but instead of a police agency symbol on the shoulder patch they had a skull and a pair of crossed hospital crutches.

He did not bother with dissolving the bodies of his victims. In fact, the corpses of eleven of his own men were dumped on Rosarito Beach with their tongues cut out as a warning to others. They were thought to have been caught snitching, though one reporter said that *El Muletas* was simply tired of hearing them moaning about their gambling debts. Nine were found in plastic bags with their heads cut off. It was thought that López Uriarte had got the idea from the beheadings in Iraq.

García Simental was so feared that his picture did not appear on billboards showing Tijuana's most wanted kidnappers. The only picture of him appeared on an FBI website which did not carry his name. Police officers, prosecutors and ordinary citizens fell silent when his name was mentioned, because García Simental had turned the kidnapping of doctors, politicians and businessmen into a multi-million dollar industry.

His alliance with the Sinaloa Cartel forced the remainder of the Arellano-Félix Organization to align themselves with the Beltrán Leyva brothers, *Los Zetas* and Vicente Carrillo Fuentes, head of the Juárez Cartel. In the ensuing war, forty-two policemen were killed, some 1,500 people died and many moved out of Tijuana to avoid being kidnapped.

The police could do nothing and the police chief was fired after federal investigators arrived in Tijuana from

diamond and two corpses were hung from an overpass. Others had been doused with gasoline and set aflame. García Simental's gunmen also shot up a billiard hall, nightclubs, a motorcycle shop and seafood restaurants.

His main line of business was kidnapping, however, and he kept his victims in cages in a network of hideouts. Henchmen were paid $400 a week to guard the prisoners and to mix up the barrels of caustic chemicals used to dispose of some of his other victims. His lieutenant, Santiago Meza López aka *El Pozolero* – 'The Stew-maker' – admitted to disposing of over three hundred bodies this way. One Mexican law enforcement official said García Simental himself liked to kill people at parties and took pleasure in their stunned reactions.

'Criminals earn respect and credibility with creative killing methods,' one official, who requested anonymity for reasons of security, told the *Los Angeles Times*. 'Your status is based on your capacity to commit the most sadistic acts. Burning corpses, using acid,

Mexico City and administered lie-detector, urinalysis and personal wealth tests to the entire police force. Ninety per cent of the officers failed outright and only four per cent were recommended for duty.

Although García Simental remained a shadowy figure, the bloodshed in Tijuana attracted the attention of President Calderón, who sent 45,000 troops to confront the cartels in his war against the traffickers. The DEA also put a $2 million bounty on his head.

Acting on intelligence supplied by the DEA, the Mexican authorities spent five months tracking down García Simental and then staged a dawn raid at his home in the city of La Paz on the Baja California peninsula. He was taken prisoner at the luxury apartment complex at Fidepaz without a shot being fired. The heavily-set prisoner had close-cropped hair and a goatee beard. He scowled as he was paraded in front of the TV cameras. Along with the prize captive, the police had seized a dozen handguns, several laptop computers and bundles of cash.

The captured laptops and García Simental's nineteen mobile phones led to the arrest of twelve more cartel suspects in two raids in late January. These included two men and a woman who were about to dissolve a body in a bathtub with chemicals.

A former Tijuana policeman who allegedly ran at least ten criminal cells for García Simental was also captured. Soon after, López Uriarte was arrested in the Indeco neighbourhood of La Paz. He was billed by the police as *El Teo*'s successor and 'leader of the Sinaloa cartel in Baja California'.

It was thought that the arrest of *El Teo* and López Uriarte had been engineered under an agreement between police chief Julián Leyzaola and Sánchez Arellano. Relative peace then returned to the area. With the Sinaloa Cartel engaged in a war with *Los Zetas* and the Juárez Cartel, it seemed they did not have the strength to take on the Tijuana Cartel as well. Instead, they humbly paid a *piso* – or 'toll' – to ship drugs through AFO territory.

Death of a Drug Baron

Francisco Rafael Arellano Félix was never the leader of the Arellano-Félix Organization. But he was key to the Tijuana Cartel's drug-running operation and he set up the deals across the border with distributor Ramón Torresillos-Rendón. He was then identified as a major drug smuggler by the DEA. This led to his arrest in 1980 and the six-year prison sentence he served in the United States following his extradition in 2006. However, taking into consideration the time he had already served, he was released on 4 March 2008, when he was deported back to Mexico.

He returned to live in some style in Los Cabos, Baya California Sur. To celebrate his sixty-third birthday, his wife and children held a party in the banqueting hall of the Hotel Marbella. Celebrities turned out, including the local mayor. Then a man dressed like a clown turned up. He walked into the ballroom and shot Francisco Rafael twice – once in the head and once in the chest. As guests scattered, the assassin made a clean getaway in an SUV waiting outside.

Numerous theories about who killed him have emerged. Manuel Aguirre Galindo, aka *El Caballo* – 'The Horse' – who had been a fugitive for more than twenty years, was arrested soon after. The authorities believe that Rafael Arellano Félix was assassinated by the Beltrán-Leyva Cartel, who were fighting over the drug-smuggling routes through Baja California. Or *El Chapo* Guzmán may have been taking his revenge. He had narrowly missed being killed by the police in Los Cabos early that year. Local drug dealers were also thought to have been involved.

It was possible that the assassination was carried out with the collaboration of the Tijuana Cartel. There was no security at the hotel, which was usually closed for such private events. Most of the guests fled, leaving the staff of the hotel and their families to give statements. Few could even agree on what the assassin was wearing.

A fleeting image was captured on a mobile phone, showing a figure who looked like a clown with a wig and a red nose. Afterwards a video of the murder was uploaded on to YouTube. On it, a shot is heard, but the music plays on and no one takes much notice. Then further shots are heard. The music stops and the guests start screaming. The authorities in Baja California Sur believe that a bald man in the video identified Francisco Rafael as the target, but no one has been arrested. As yet, the case remains open.

A member of the Federal Investigative Agency scans passing traffic for suspicious activity in the wake of further severe violence from members of the drug cartels, 2005

THE SINALOA CARTEL

Joaquín Archivaldo Guzmán Loera, aka *El Chapo* – 'Shorty' – remained loyal when his boss Félix Gallardo went to jail, visiting him several times.

He was also well positioned to take over the lion's share of the drug trafficking business. Though the centre of his operations was in Agua Prieta in the northeast corner of the border state of Sonora, he lived in Guadalajara where he could stay close to *El Padrino*. Like his mentor, he had bought anonymous houses in residential areas in Culiacán, Mexicali, Tecate and Guadalajara, along with a number of places in Mexico City. These would be used to house drugs, guns, cash and any number of his men. He also bought ranches in Sinaloa, Sonora, Chihuahua and Durango,

The arrest of El Chapo, aged 55, perhaps the most powerful drug overlord in the world. The Archbishop of Durango had said of him, 'He is omnipresent... he is everywhere'. Now he is in jail

where local *gomeros* would grow poppies and marijuana.

Unlike other drug barons, Guzmán Loera did not confine himself to one smuggling hub. Instead, he would roam the country with a convoy of henchmen making alliances with local *caciques*, or strongmen. Once the Colombian cocaine route through the Caribbean and south Florida was closed by Operation Hat Trick, the Colombians found they could only transport drugs as far north as Chiapas in Guatemala, which bordered southern Mexico. So *El Chapo* made a deal with Pedro Díaz Parada, the local strongman in Oaxaca.

Guzmán Loera also bought aircraft – or stole them, even from the government – to fly the drugs northwards. Otherwise drugs would be transported in the false

United States Customs officials found a 6.6 lb (3 kg) statue of Christ filled with cocaine in the trunk of a car

bottoms of trucks. Indeed, he demonstrated remarkable ingenuity. Drugs were stuffed into beer cases, shoes, dolls, surfboards and people. A woman with a protruding belly was stopped in Tijuana when it was found that she was not pregnant. Instead, she was carrying several pounds of tightly wrapped cocaine. Another woman carried cocaine that had been surgically implanted in her buttocks. She died of blood poisoning when the container burst at Mexico City airport.

At Tecate, Baja California, cocaine was found concealed in cans of chili peppers and in 2008 United States Customs officials found a cocaine-filled (6.6 lb) 3 kg plaster statue of Jesus in the trunk of a car on its way over the border into Laredo.

Guzmán Loera was a man who liked to enjoy his money and did not oversee the minutiae of every drug deal. With two other former Gallardo lieutenants, Adrián Gómez González and Héctor Luis Palma Salazar, he formed the Sinaloa Cartel which became Mexico's largest drug-smuggling operation.

Tip-off

In May 1990, United States Customs officials received a tip-off about a warehouse in Douglas, Arizona, directly across the border from Agua Prieta. When they raided it, they found 2,037 lbs (924 kg) of cocaine. Later, they found what they dubbed 'Cocaine Alley', after lifting a steel drainage grate and then jack-hammering through a concrete panel. This was a two-hundred-foot (60 m) passageway that ran from the warehouse to *El Chapo's* attorney's house in Agua Prieta. It had air-conditioning, electric lighting and a drainage system.

Normally the tunnel was opened by a spigot. This operated a hydraulic system that raised the false floor under the pool table. A pulley was used to lower the drugs on to a cart that ran on rails below. Along the tunnel there were side rooms used to store drugs, weapons and cash.

Later, another tunnel was discovered. This ran 1,452 feet (443 m) from a house in Tijuana to a warehouse over the border that belonged to the same people who had been importing the chili. The miners who had dug the tunnels had been press-ganged into the task. They were forced to live below ground during the construction and when the tunnel was completed they were killed.

Arrest and Escape

El Chapo was arrested in 1991, but after pulling $50,000 from a suitcase he walked free. On another occasion, he gave a police *comandante* $1 million and five Dodge Ramchargers to look the other way when two planes filled with drugs landed in Jalisco.

In 1993, he was held in Guatemala in connection with the murder of Cardinal Posadas Ocampo. Then he was extradited to Mexico, where he was sentenced to twenty years for drug trafficking, bribery and criminal association. The murder charges were dropped and he was given a luxurious cell, where he imbibed fine wines and gave interviews to CBS news anchor Dan Rather and other media mavens. He even had a love affair behind bars with inmate and former police officer Zulema Julieta Hernández.

While in jail, he maintained contact with the Beltrán Leyva brothers, who had formed a cartel of their own. It was plain that he was still in the trafficking business.

In 2000, lawyer José Antonio Ortega Sanchez came to interview Guzmán Loera on behalf of the government. The interview was scheduled for 10 am. Ortega Sanchez arrived on time, but a guard told him that *El Chapo* had been delayed. He waited and waited. Guzmán Loera eventually showed up at 11 pm. He apologized, saying that he had had a conjugal visit.

Arturo Beltrán Leyva was part of the council of war held to discuss how to deal with rival cartels

'Afterwards I took a bath,' he said. 'Then I had a short nap… in order to be ready for you.'

Over coffee and a selection of cakes Guzmán Loera spoke for five hours, never taking his eyes off the questioner, even when he was plainly lying or, at least, contradicting previous testimony.

Even when he was in jail, *El Chapo* was not slow to spot a new business opportunity. The largest suppliers of methamphetamine were the Amezcua Contreras brothers – Adán, Luis and Jesús – who formed the Colima Cartel in 1988. But they did not have the political protection other narcos enjoyed and found themselves in jail in the late 1990s. *El Chapo* and *El Mayo* already had the distribution system to ship marijuana and cocaine, so they simply added crystal meth to the manifest.

When Guzmán Loera faced extradition to the United States in 2001, he gave up this life of luxury in jail. The official story is that he befriended a prison maintenance worker named Javier Camberos. *El Chapo* told the guards – who were on his payroll – that Camberos was going to smuggle some gold out of the jail in a laundry basket, which they were not to search. Guzmán Loera then hid in the laundry basket and was wheeled out of the jail. However, most observers believe that Guzmán Loera was simply allowed to walk out, because the electronically controlled door of his cell inexplicably flew open and the CCTV tapes for that night seem to have been mysteriously erased.

The incident was known as the 'golden kilogram', because that is the amount of gold *El Chapo* is thought to have spread around in bribes. He once boasted that he spent $5 million a month while he was in jail. Following his escape, a federal investigation led to the arrest of seventy-one prison officials.

Back in Action

In Monterrey, Guzmán Loera met up with '*El Mayo*' Zambada García, '*El Azul*' Esparragoza Moreno and Arturo Beltrán Leyva. There were weighty matters on the agenda – how to curtail the growing power of the Tijuana Cartel; how to clip the wings of the Carrillo Fuentes family in Ciudad Juárez; and how to challenge the Zetas. Information concerning the whereabouts of Benjamín Arellano Félix was given to the authorities and he was

Nine bodies found hanging from a bridge in Nuevo Laredo, Mexico on 4 May 2012: Mexican authorities announced that the victims were five men and four women suspected of being members of Los Zetas drugs cartel. They had been tortured

The Battle for Nuevo Laredo

Nuevo Laredo in the state of Tamaulipas lies across the Rio Grande from Laredo in Texas and is one of the Mexican crime cartels' gateways to the United States. It is Mexico's largest inland port and a centre of trucking. By 2005, more than 77 per cent of the cocaine and 70 per cent of the crystal meth sold in the United States passed through Nuevo Laredo.

Nuevo Laredo was under the control of the Gulf Cartel, but the rival Sinaloa Cartel tried to assume control when Osiel Cárdenas Guillén was arrested in March 2003. Its leader, Joaquín Guzmán Loera – *El Chapo* – sent a young lieutenant named Édgar Valdéz Villarreal – *La Barbie* – to take over. Soon after, Valdéz and Arturo Beltrán Leyva delivered a $1.5-million bribe to the commander of the Federal Investigations Agency, Domingo Gonzalez Díaz, for his protection during the struggle against their rivals. The Gulf Cartel's response was to gun down the federal commander in Nuevo Laredo, along with his brother, only hours after he had taken office.

Within days of Gonzalez Díaz's assassination, the United States closed its consulate in Nuevo Laredo, comparing the town to Baghdad at the height of the Iraq War – the rival cartels were fighting it out with machine guns, grenades and bazookas in broad daylight. Over the next two years more than two thousand lay dead in the streets of Nuevo Laredo.

While Cárdenas continued running his gang from inside La Palma, the maximum security prison, the Nuevo Laredo police department was almost entirely at his disposal with the federal forces not only protecting the Gulf Cartel, but also kidnapping and killing its rivals. In 2005, not one of the town's four hundred officially recorded murders was solved. Most went unreported.

After a battle in 2006, a bystander saw men with assault rifles throwing bodies into the backs of trucks and SUVs. The corpses were disposed of on the outskirts of the city, where they were dissolved in vats of acid, minced up and fed to animals or incinerated with gas so all evidence of them disappeared. Sometimes there was a very public murder to make a point. The dead body of Dionisio 'El Chacho' Ramón García, leader of the local *Los Chachos* – 'The Lads' – gang which was allied to the Sinaloa Cartel, was left out on public display dressed in women's underwear for everyone to see.

Spearheaded by *Los Zetas*, thirty or so deserters from Mexico's Special Forces, the Gulf Cartel began to get the upper hand. They hung out *narcomantas* – narco message banners – asking the Sinaloa Cartel: 'What even could you want? The state of Tamaulipas, Mexico, the United States, the whole world – Territory of the Gulf Cartel.'

But by 2010 the fighting had abated.

'There has been a truce,' said human rights campaigner Raymundo Ramos Vásquez. 'I don't know the details, and I don't want to know them, but the Gulf Cartel has won, the Sinaloa Cartel has lost, and they have reached an accord. I can only guess that Guzmán pays some kind of tax to use the corridor, if he uses it at all. The Gulf Cartel controls the corridor again, and the federal army patrols every block of the city, twenty-four hours a day, three hundred and sixty-five days a year. Apart from a new presence, *La Familia*, this has stopped the war.'

The *Pax Mafioso* was enforced by *Los Zetas*, who ran the city by fear, threatening the police, journalists and city officials, and extorting money from businesses.

However, in April 2012 the fighting broke out again. Fourteen mutilated bodies were found in a car left in the city centre. The following month, the bodies of five men and four women were found hanging from the overpass to the main highway, alongside a menacing *narcomanta*. The victims had been beaten and tortured. Their faces were wrapped in duct tape, their wrists were bound and as a further humiliation some had their trousers pulled down.

Hours later, the police found fourteen human heads in a cooler outside city hall. The fourteen bodies were found in black plastic bags inside a car abandoned near the World Trade Bridge that connects Nuevo Laredo to its sister city, Laredo, Texas.

The killings had restarted because the Sinaloa Cartel had joined forces with the Gulf Cartel to take on *Los Zetas*, who had formed a cartel of their own. The victims of the horrific new attacks were thought to be Zetas and the perpetrators the Sinaloa Cartel. A message delivered with the severed heads and allegedly signed by Guzmán said the Sinaloa Cartel was now back in Nuevo Laredo to clean up the city.

Nevertheless the Zetas hung on until their leader Miguel Ángel Treviño Morales, who used Nuevo Laredo as his base, was arrested in July 2013 after an American tip-off. He was taken without a shot being fired, though a number of guns and $2 million in cash were found in the car with him. The inevitable result will be more bloodshed, with Guzmán and the other cartels competing for control while Treviño's men fight it out between themselves.

Vicente Carrillo Fuentes was the third of six brothers, from a family where there were also six sisters

arrested. The youngest of the Carrillo Fuentes brothers, Rodolfo, aka *El Niño de Oro* – 'The Golden Child' – was shot and killed by fifteen *sicarios* – 'hired assassins' – in the Plaza Cinépolis in Culiacán, along with his wife Giovanna Quevedo Gastélum and a man who worked

in the parking lot. When one of Rodolfo's bodyguards was injured, he turned out to be none other than the commander of the Ministerial Police of State (PME) Pedro Pérez López. The governor gave him paid leave, praising him as an 'effective commander'.

El Mayo ended up in possession of the body. The then leader of the Carrillo Fuentes organization, Vicente Carrillo Fuentes – *El Viceroy* – telephoned him and asked: 'Are you with me or against me?'

El Mayo answered: 'I'm with you, of course.'

So *El Viceroy* asked him for the head of *El Chapo*. He did not get it. Instead, war broke out. There were clashes in the nearby towns of Bacurimi, Bellavista, Culiacancito, El Tamarindo, El Pinole and El Rosal Enfermo. Five gunmen were killed and two more were wounded and transferred to a hospital as detainees.

The next day, three corpses of the alleged killers were found stacked in an armoured truck in Navolato. One of those executed was the former commander of the PME, Jesús Antonio Sánchez Verdugo. The victims were

The Oaxaca Cartel

The Oaxaca Cartel is one of the smaller drug trafficking outfits in Mexico. It began when the 'Oaxaca boss' Pedro Díaz Parada began growing marijuana around San Pedro Totolapa in the state of Oaxaca in the 1970s. He soon became the top producer in the Isthmus of Tehuantepec, the narrowest part of Mexico.

With headquarters in Santa María Zoquitlán in Oaxaca, he moved into the neighbouring state of Chiapas at Arriaga. From there he used light aircraft and speedboats to traffic marijuana and cocaine north to Chihuahua, Durango, Tamaulipas and Veracruz, then on to Brownsville and Houston in Texas. More cocaine came in from Colombia, through Guatemala.

Díaz Parada forged an alliance with the Sinaloa Cartel, but when *El Chapo* was arrested he

shifted his allegiance to the Tijuana Cartel. He also diversified into transportation, restaurants, nightclubs and loan-sharking.

Arrested in 1985, he was sentenced to thirty-three years in jail. Turning to the judge he said: 'I will go free and you will die.'

Six days later, the *cacique* escaped from Oaxaca's Santa María Ixcotel prison and in September 1987 the judge's body was found with thirty-three bullet holes in it and a note that said: 'A bullet for every year.'

Recaptured in 1990, he escaped again in 1992. He was retaken in January 2007 while travelling in a car carrying military weapons and twenty bags of marijuana. By this time most of the cartel's four hundred members had been rounded up and *Los Zetas* were aiming to fill the gap.

carrying magazine pouches and a fragmentation grenade. They had been tied hand and foot and had been tortured before being given the *coup de grâce*.

Five members of the Sinaloa Cartel were executed in Nuevo Laredo and *El Chapo*'s brother, Arturo Guzmán Loera, aka *El Pollo* – 'The Chicken' – was killed in clashes within the maximum security prison at La Palma.

Two months after Rodolfo Carrillo Fuentes was killed, two hundred paramilitaries in Blackhawk helicopters swooped down on *El Chapo*'s stronghold in the Sierra Madre mountains, in the so-called Golden Triangle: a desolate patch between Culiacán and the neighbouring Durango and Chihuahua states. His voice had been heard on the phone half an hour before. All they could do was blow up his Dodge Ram pick-up and his Hummer. The man himself had long gone.

El Chapo's brother, son, two nephews and a niece were apprehended in June 2005, but the drug lord still dared to appear in public. In November, diners in a busy restaurant in Culiacán were told to remain in their seats. The doors would be locked and no one would be allowed to leave – or use their mobile phones. But they were not to worry and should continue to eat as normal. And they were not to pay the bill – 'the boss' would pay.

Then fifteen men came in carrying AK-47s. Next *El Chapo* arrived. He went around shaking hands and saying: 'Hello, I'm Joaquín Guzmán. How nice to meet you.'

He then disappeared into a back room to eat. Two hours later, he made his way discreetly out of the back door, followed by his trigger-men. This happened more than once. However, after he made a provocative appearance at the Aroma Restaurant in Ciudad Juárez, the building was torched.

In 2007, the middle-aged Guzmán Loera became enamoured of 17-year-old Emma Coronel, a contestant for the 'Queen of the Great Guayaba and Coffee Festival' held at Angostura, Sinaloa. He reportedly employed a ghostwriter to pen love letters. To support her candidacy, Senorita Coronel Aispuro sponsored a dance. That day, black-hooded armed men arrived on motorcycles and sealed off the town. Then a plane landed carrying Los Canelos de Durango, a popular local band.

Another five planes followed. One was carrying a smart but casually dressed *El Chapo* with an AK-47 strapped across his chest and weapons that matched his clothes

Ines Coronel Barreras, El Chapo's father-in-law, was seized by Mexican authorities in 2013, along with four automatic rifles, a handgun and more than 550 lbs (250 kilos) of marijuana

tucked into his belt. With him was Emma Coronel's uncle, Ignacio 'Nacho' Coronel Villarreal, head of the Jalisco Cartel.

As the band played Emma and Joaquín's favourite song 'Cruzando Cerros y Arroyos', her parents beamed. Six months later, on Emma's eighteenth birthday, the couple were wed. They left on their honeymoon a day before a military squad reached Angostura. The United States put a $5 million bounty on *El Chapo*'s head, while the Mexican government offered another thirty million pesos for information that would lead to his capture.

Édgar Valdéz Villarreal had lots of contacts in the US which made him a very useful man for the drug cartels

Édgar Valdéz Villarreal

Born in Laredo, Texas in 1973, Édgar Valdéz Villarreal is known as *La Barbie* because his light complexion and blue eyes make him look like Ken, the Barbie doll's male companion. Raised on the United States side of the border, he grew up in a middle-class district popular with police officers, firefighters and Border Patrol agents. His father owned a bar and nightclub in Laredo.

A linebacker in Laredo United High School's football team, Valdéz was arrested at the age of nineteen for running down a middle school counsellor with his truck while speeding down a street in Laredo. While he was charged with negligent homicide he was never sentenced. However, he had a criminal record for petty offences such as speeding, drunken driving and public intoxication.

A small-time drug dealer, he fled to Mexico to avoid being arrested for distributing marijuana. There he rose to become head of a team of assassins in the Beltrán-Leyva gang and bodyguard to Arturo Beltrán Leyva himself, finally becoming head of the cartel's operations in Acapulco.

As head of the *Los Negros* faction, he led the Sinaloa Cartel's efforts to take over Nuevo Laredo. A raid on his home revealed automatic weapons, grenades and police uniforms. His name appeared on the most wanted lists on both sides of the border and there was a combined reward of $4 million on his head. In spite of this, he took out a full-page advertisement in *El Norte* to protest his innocence, claiming that he was a legitimate businessman who was pestered for bribes by the police. He remained an illegal immigrant, though.

After being pursued across five states, he was finally arrested in August 2010. However, life behind bars is not too odious. A surprise search of the jail in Acapulco uncovered nineteen prostitutes, numerous bottles of booze, two sacks of marijuana, a dozen television sets, a hundred fighting cocks and two peacocks that the prisoners kept as pets.

Cartels at War

Having declared war on the Juárez Cartel, the Sinaloa Cartel also broke with the Beltrán Leyva brothers. According to the DEA, they were competing over the allegiance of a cell in Chicago, a lucrative part of the market, when *El Chapo* engineered the arrest of Alfredo Beltrán Leyva – aka *El Mochomo* after a variety of fighting ant – in January 2008. Dozens of people were killed as the fighting escalated.

At 8:30 pm on 8 May 2008, *El Chapo*'s 22-year-old son Édgar Guzmán López was walking across the car park of City Club, a wholesale store, when three cars carrying more than a dozen gunmen approached. Guzmán and his companion ran for their trucks, one of which was armoured. More than five hundred bullets were fired; the attackers had even brought a bazooka. Twenty cars were shot up and Édgar Guzmán and his colleague Arturo Cazares lay dead.

During May, 116 people died in Culiacán, 26 of them policemen. In June, 128 died; in July, 143. General Noe Sandoval Alcazar, who was based there, was given two thousand extra troops to quell the violence. Banners appeared saying: 'This is Beltrán Leyva territory' and '*Chapo*, you will fall'. *Narcomantas* also accused *El Mayo* and *El Chapo* of making a deal with the federal government to take over the entire narcotics smuggling business.

Even the Church has tried to speak out against *El Chapo*. In April 2009 the Archbishop of Durango, Héctor Gonzáles Martinez, held a press conference denouncing threats made against his priests by the Sinaloa Cartel and *La Familia Michoacana*. In it he said: 'Further up from Guanaceví' – in the rugged Sierra Madre mountains of northern Durango – '*El Chapo* Guzmán lives over there, but, well, we all know this, except for the authorities.'

Asked whether he had made a formal statement to the authorities, the archbishop said: 'We are all convinced that it would not have much effect.'

The following day, the newspapers that carried the statement quickly sold out to 'unknown agents'. The local media did not print the archbishop's reply and the federal government threatened to arrest him for refusing to make a formal statement, though they later backed off.

Meanwhile the governor of Durango declined to accept any responsibility for the archbishop's safety.

Four days after the interview, the bodies of two murdered army officers were found in Guanaceví. In regular narco fashion a note was left with the bodies. It read: 'Neither priests or the authorities will ever get *El Chapo*.'

Mexico's assistant attorney general claimed that Guzmán Loera had nearly been captured in February 2009, while staying in a million-dollar home overlooking the Gulf of California in Los Cabos, at the tip of the Baja peninsula. Teodoro García Simental and Francisco Javier Arellano Félix had been arrested nearby. But only four people were found in the house where Guzmán Loera was thought to have been staying. Diplomatic cables released by WikiLeaks said that he was usually surrounded by a security detail of up to three hundred men as he moved between ten to fifteen locations to avoid capture. He had also been seen in Argentina and Guatemala.

In August 2011, Guzmán Loera's new wife Emma, a United States citizen, crossed the border into California where she gave birth to twin girls. Her father, Ines Coronel Barreras, was arrested in 2013 for growing marijuana and smuggling it to Arizona. The United States Treasury said he was a 'key operative' of the Sinaloa Cartel.

United States federal agents said that while Emma Coronel could provide information on her husband's whereabouts, the problem with apprehending him was how the Mexican authorities could seize him when he was surrounded by such a large band of well-armed men.

Finally, after 13 years on the run, *El Chapo* let his guard drop. He was captured in the early morning of 22 February 2014 in a nondescript holiday apartment block in the Pacific resort of Mazatlán during a joint operation conducted by the DEA and the Mexican Navy. The authorities had been closing in on him for some time, using cellphone and other data. They had already uncovered his network of seven safe houses in Culiacán, connected by secret passages and protected by reinforced steel doors.

On the morning of the arrest, while *El Chapo*, his beauty queen wife, their 2-year-old twins and the bodyguard all slept, Mexican marines used infrared and bodyheat scanners to locate their quarry, before smashing in the door of the 'no frills beachside condo' where they were staying. The marines had their man in handcuffs before he could reach for his AK-47. Not a shot was fired.

Ciudad Juárez, often known as just Juárez, has been called 'the most violent zone in the world outside declared war zones':
in 2009 the murder rate was 132 per 100,000 citizens, the worst in the world at the time

THE JUÁREZ CARTEL

In the early 1980s, competing factions fought over the drug route between Ciudad Juárez and El Paso. Félix Gallardo's right hand man *Don Neto* Fonseca Carrillo sent former police chief Rafael Aguilar Guajardo to contact Pablo Acosta Villarreal, who operated out of the dusty border town of Ojinaga, Chihuahua, and controlled 250 miles (400 km) of the border – shipping, it was estimated, sixty tons of cocaine into the United States each year.

Known as '*El Pablote*', 'The Czar', 'The Ojinaga Fox', 'The Ojinaga Godfather' and 'The Ojinaga Robin Hood', Acosta Villarreal helped the poor in Ojinaga, buying school books for working-class students and sometimes even paying for their university or private school tuition. He was also said to be one of a new breed of narco-trafficker – flamboyant, openly defiant of authority, impulsive and unpredictably violent. Often boasting of payoffs and murders, he would

do anything to consolidate his power. He had a penchant for fine Texan Stetsons, AR-15 machine guns, brand-new Ford Broncos, drinking tequila, snorting cocaine and smoking Marlboro cigarettes laced with crack cocaine.

In April 1987, Acosta Villarreal was killed in an ambush orchestrated by the FBI. Aguilar Guajardo took over, aided by Amado Carrillo Fuentes, *Don Neto*'s nephew. Carrillo Fuentes negotiated deals with the Medellín and Cali Cartels, but he soon experienced something of a setback when he was arrested in Guadalajara. He did not implicate *Don Neto* or any of the other bosses of the loose federation formed by Félix Gallardo, but just admitted to smuggling some marijuana with the late Acosta Villarreal. Although several of his aeroplanes were confiscated, he only spent a few weeks in jail for the possession of illegal weapons and public health offences before the charges were dropped.

Lord of the Skies

In 1993, Aguilar Guajardo was killed and Amado Carrillo Fuentes took his place as head of the Juárez Cartel. Using a fleet of Boeing 727s to transport drugs, Carrillo Fuentes became known as *El Señor de Los Cielos* – 'Lord of the Skies'. At its height, the Juárez Cartel was trafficking four times more cocaine into the United States than any other trafficker. It was making billions of dollars, with each major shipment yielding $20 to $30 million to the Colombians.

Carrillo Fuentes even co-opted President Zedillo's drug czar General Gutiérrez Rebollo. While cracking down hard on the Arellano-Félix Organization and other rivals of the Juárez Cartel, he went easy on Carrillo Fuentes, who claimed that by only selling drugs in the United States and Europe, not in Mexico itself, he was helping the government eliminate 'unorganized narcotics trafficking'.

A cavalry officer, General Gutiérrez Rebollo bought alfalfa from a farm owned by one of Carrillo Fuentes' top aides. After the farmer's son was wounded by an AFO gunman he decided to tell the general all he knew about the Arellano-Félix Organization. This allowed Gutiérrez Rebollo to send hundreds of soldiers sweeping through Tijuana in a clean-up that won him accolades. Meanwhile he was living high in Guadalajara, amassing a fleet of cars and armoured Jeeps, along with two thoroughbreds, and using soldiers as cooks, drivers and gardeners at his wife's household as well as the homes of his two mistresses.

General Gutiérrez Rebollo was not Carrillo Fuentes' only military contact. In 1966, an Air Force flight specialist admitted directing the trafficker's planes into Guadalajara airports. Four other senior officers involved in intelligence, counter-insurgency and repression were also arrested.

Despite his high-ranking contacts, Carrillo Fuentes decided that he needed plastic surgery on his face and liposuction to change his body shape. He died during the operation. The bodies of the two surgeons, along with a third unidentified corpse, were found embedded in barrels of concrete beside a highway in Mexico City. The surgeons had been bound and gagged, and showed signs of torture. Their fingernails had been torn out, they were covered in burns and they had been strangled with cables. The third person had been shot.

Carrillo Fuentes received a costly funeral in his home village of Guamuchilito in Sinaloa, where he was hailed as another 'Robin Hood'. He had given cattle, cash and cars to local people. The authorities in Juárez said he had never done anything wrong there, so there were no outstanding warrants. Mexican newspapers published pictures of him in Jerusalem with a priest. He was also said to have generously given *narcolimosnas* – 'narco-alms' – to the Catholic Church.

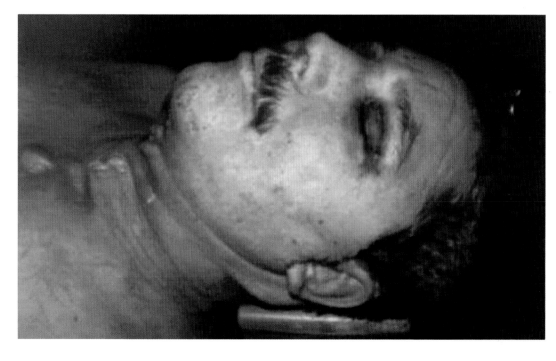

This photograph, published in the Mexican newspaper Sol de Culiacán, *shows Amado Carrillo Fuentes who died shortly after plastic surgery*

Two men mop up the blood-stained patio where 16 young people were murdered in 2010

The Atrocities of *La Línea*

The cops-turned-killers of *La Línea* first surfaced when Chihuahua's attorney general accused them of torturing and killing Benjamín LeBarón, leader of the polygamous Mormon community at Galeana, who had spoken out against the cartels. On 7 July 2009 he was seized by ten armed men and beaten in front of his family. After one of his brothers-in-law intervened, both men were found shot dead. *La Línea* denied the killings, blaming the Sinaloa Cartel.

Then on 31 January 2010 some youngsters were having a birthday party in Villas de Salvárcar, a working-class neighbourhood of Ciudad Juárez, when seven cars with tinted windows closed the street and blocked the exits. Sixteen victims, aged fifteen to twenty, were killed and more than a hundred rounds from AK-47s were found at the scene. Four days after the massacre a lookout named José Dolores Arroyo Chavarría said that some twenty-four gunmen had been told to kill everyone inside. The following year four men were sentenced to 240 years each in connection with the murders.

In another incident, on 10 June 2010, six vehicles turned up outside the Life and Faith church-run rehabilitation clinic in Chihuahua City. Men carrying AR-15 and AK-47 assault rifles and wearing ski masks and protective gear jumped out. After lining the patients up outside they shot them, killing nineteen and wounding four. The pastor said that some of the victims were former members of *Los Mexicles*, a gang that works alongside *Artistas Asesinos*, an armed wing of the Sinaloa Cartel.

A few days later, on 16 June 2010, members of *La Línea* dumped an injured man dressed in a police uniform on the sidewalk in Ciudad Juárez and called the police. When a policeman and a paramedic arrived they set off a car bomb, which killed them instantly. The injured man, who was not a policeman, and a bystander were also killed. Footage of the bombing showing two federal policemen on fire was aired on national TV.

Finally, on 23 October 2010 gunmen raided another teenager's birthday party in the Horizontes del Sur in Ciudad Juárez, just a mile from Villas de Salvárcar. After securing the area by blocking the traffic, they fired over seventy rounds, killing thirteen victims aged between fourteen and twenty and injuring more than twenty others – one only nine years old.

The Viceroy

Amado Carrillo Fuentes' younger brother Vicente 'The Viceroy' took over after a brief turf war with Rafael Muñoz Talavera, who was found dead in the back seat of a 1985 Jeep Cherokee in a middle-class area of Ciudad Juárez in September 1998. His hands were bound and there were four shots to his head and his heart. He was one of the sixty-five people killed in the infighting.

Although he had served time on drugs charges, Muñoz Talavera said that he was a 'simple, hardworking man' with no connection to trafficking. He once wrote to President Zedillo, complaining about 'a group of criminals

Another victim of drug violence lies next to his crumpled car in Juárez. In 2009 they reinforced the police force with thousands of federal troops and the crime wave slowly began to recede

in the city that wants to kidnap members of my family'. They wanted 'to pressure me because they think I'm competing in their dirty business', he said. He also ran the text of the letter as an advertisement in local newspapers. Plainly it did no good.

In 2001, top trafficker Alcides *El Metro* Ramón Magaña was arrested in the Gulf Coast state of Tabasco. He would fly drugs up from Colombia to covert airstrips in Central America, using lightweight aircraft that eluded radar. From there, they were ferried in small launches or *pangas* to Chetumal, Quintana Roo. Then tankers and trucks took them to the United States via Reynosa.

It is thought that *El Metro* enjoyed the co-operation of Mario Villanueva Madrid, the governor of Quintana Roo – until he failed to turn up to the inauguration of his successor in March 1999. Also known as 'the Crooked One' – though this could be a reference to his partially

LEFT *Governor of Quintana Roo, Mario Villanueva Madrid, was a man on the take*

BELOW *The bodies of six victims of the Juárez Cartel are taken away. They were discovered in a mass grave*

paralyzed face – Villanueva Madrid was thought to have received $400,000 to $500,000 in cash for each 500- to 1,000-kilogram shipment of cocaine. He was arrested in May 2001 and jailed for money laundering and trafficking in both Mexico and the United States.

In the late 1990s, the Juárez Cartel was the principal target of the 'Maxiprocesso' effort, which issued 110 arrest warrants for the arrest of alleged cartel members and accomplices. Sixty-five of them were executed against persons allegedly tied to the Juárez Cartel. During the trials, it was revealed that Amado Carrillo Fuentes had little confidence in his brother Vicente. He thought him unintelligent. A flamboyant character, Vicente 'The Viceroy' enjoyed executing enemies, drinking rum, taking drugs, visiting strip clubs, driving flashy cars, buying gaudy mansions, surrounding himself with bodyguards and chasing women. He once offered a $200,000 reward to anyone who killed a DEA agent on Mexican territory.

Soon he was wanted for numerous crimes across

southeast Texas. In 2003, the FBI traced him to a house in El Paso, but failed to capture him. After the war with the Sinaloa Cartel sparked by the murder of Rodolfo Carrillo Fuentes, Vincente dropped out of sight and was thought to be hiding in Lerdo, Durango, where he had three houses. His accomplice, the Juárez Cartel's top gunman Arturo *El Chaky* González Hernández, who also hid out there, was arrested in April 2005.

The New Generation

Ricardo García Urquiza, aka 'The Doctor', as he had once been a medical student, was left running the cartel. He was one of a 'new generation' of drug lords who liked to keep a low profile, unlike the flamboyant kingpins of the past.

'He could walk down the street and you would think he's a banker,' said a United States official.

Using encrypted emails, satellite communications and other state-of-the-art technology, he devised two new drug trafficking routes. There was a Pacific route where the drugs were shipped from Colombia to the Galapagos Islands, which belong to Ecuador. From there they travelled up the coast of Central America until they reached Oaxaca, Michoacán and Guerrero. The Caribbean corridor started at the ports of Cartagena, Barranquilla and Santa Maria in Colombia. The drugs then took a tortuous route through Panama, Costa Rica, Puerto Rico, the Dominican Republic, Guatemala, Nicaragua, Honduras, Jamaica, the Cayman Islands and Belize,

Ricardo García Urquiza, aka 'The Doctor', ran a hi-tech operation and kept a low profile

Gente Nueva

The *Gente Nueva* – or 'New People' – were formed in 2007 as the main arm of the Sinaloa Cartel in Ciudad Juárez. They were pitted against the Juárez Cartel's allies *La Línea* and *Los Aztecas*. The *Gente Nueva* themselves were allied to *Artistas Asesinos* and *Los Mexicles*. In four years, the war left over ten thousand dead.

In August 2009, the *Gente Nueva* killed eight people in the 7&7 Bar. A few weeks later they stormed the El Aliviane drug rehabilitation centre, lined the patients up against the wall and gunned down twenty of them. The following year the *Gente Nueva*'s leader José Antonio Torres Marrufo was arrested for ordering the massacre.

As the fighting in Ciudad Juárez declined, the *Gente Nueva* moved on to fight in Durango, where messages warned rivals that they had twenty-four hours to leave the state or be killed. The *Gente Nueva* were thought to have been responsible for mass graves found there.

In Veracruz, gunmen blocked a major street with two trucks carrying thirty-five bodies and a message which read:

'No more extortions or murders of innocent people! People of Veracruz, do not allow extortions; do not pay for protection. This is going to happen to all the Zetas-f**ks that continue to operate in Veracruz. This territory has a new proprietor – G.N.'

But there is some doubt that the *Gente Nueva* were responsible as the Jalisco New Generation Cartel also claimed responsibility.

before finally entering Mexico through Quintana Roo.

García Urquiza was seized in a Mexico City shopping mall in November 2005. He was picked up along with his brother Jesus Omar and Maria Nereida Garcia, a suspected cartel accountant, who was arrested leaving her home with nearly $3 million in cash. Gilberto Lugo, who ran the cartel's North Texas operation, had pleaded guilty to federal charges the previous month, along with seven other men.

The war between the Sinaloa and Juárez Cartels peaked in 2008 when around 1,600 people were found dead in Ciudad Juárez. The bloodletting was curtailed in March when President Calderón sent in five thousand more troops and hundreds of additional federal police.

In April 2009, Amado Carrillo Fuentes' son Vicente Carrillo Leyva was arrested while out jogging in an Abercrombie & Fitch warm-up suit in Mexico's wealthy Bosques de las Lomas area, where he was living under the name Alejandro Peralta Álvarez. Neighbours thought he was a regular businessman and said he was 'discreet and friendly'. Carrillo Leyva is one of the new breed of *cachorros* or 'narco-puppies', who wear Armani suits, live in exclusive residence neighbourhoods, mix with the elite and master the latest technology.

Assistant Prosecutor Marisela Morales said Carrillo Leyva was 'considered one of the heirs to the criminal organization known as the Juárez Cartel, after the death of his father, Amado Carrillo Fuentes'.

The Mexican government had put a bounty of thirty million pesos – $2.16 million – on Carrillo Leyva's head. Nevertheless he was acquitted on money-laundering charges, though he remained in jail for the illegal possession of firearms. Then in December 2010 he was released after paying bail of 160,000 pesos – around $12,000. The judge said there was not enough evidence to keep him in custody. The only charge left against him was one of using fake ID papers – but this was common practice in Mexico. Nevertheless, the federal government came up with new money-laundering charges, so as he walked out of Almoloya de Juárez maximum security prison he was grabbed by the federal police and flown by helicopter to the dungeons of *Subprocuraduría de Investigación Especializada en Delincuencia Organizada* (SIEDO) – the Assistant Attorney General's Office for the

LEFT *Police deal with the bodies of seven men gunned down in Ciudad Juárez, together with narcomanta (propaganda banners from the cartels) justifying their horrific violence*

RIGHT *Vicente Carrillo Leyva belongs to a new breed of 'narco puppies' who live in exclusive neighbourhoods, mix with the elite and master the latest technology*

Special Investigation of Organized Crimes, which became SEIDO in October 2012.

Despite these setbacks, Vicente Carrillo Fuentes and Vicente Carrillo Leyva reportedly remained in control of 521 gangs in Ciudad Juárez. They set up an armed wing called *La Línea* under Juan Pablo Ledezma, aka José Luis 'JL' Fratello, to fight off the takeover of Ciudad Juárez by the Sinaloa Cartel, recruiting current and former Chihuahua policemen. As well as being responsible for a number of massacres of seemingly innocent people, they also set off a car bomb which targeted the federal police, killing four. A message scrawled on the wall of a nearby elementary school read: 'FBI and DEA. Go and investigate authorities that are giving support to the Sinaloa Cartel. If not, we will put more car bombs.' Another warned that 'what occurred ... would continue to happen to authorities that carry on supporting Shorty'.

On 25 January 2011, *narcomantas* in Ciudad Juárez announced the formation of the New Juárez Cartel. They threatened to kill a policeman each day until police chief Julián Leyzaola, a native of Culiacán, stopped supporting the Sinaloa Cartel, though it was reported that while working as police chief of Tijuana he had rejected an offer of $80,000 a week from an emissary of *El Chapo*.

This was no empty threat. Eleven policemen were killed in January alone. In September, the New Juárez Cartel released a video showing its members interrogating a prison guard who had admitted working with the Sinaloa Cartel. His body was found later. Another message from the New Juárez Cartel was left beside a dismembered body the following month, but this was not released by the authorities.

It is thought that the New Juárez Cartel is a coalition of the old Juárez Cartel, the Vicente Carrillo Fuentes Organization, *La Línea*, their allies *Los Aztecas* and the other criminal elements that oppose the Sinaloa Cartel. Meanwhile *La Línea* broke ranks and formed an alliance with *Los Zetas* and what was left of the Beltrán-Leyva Cartel, forcing the Sinaloa Cartel into an alliance with the Gulf Cartel and the remnants of *La Familia Michoacana*, forming the 'New Federation'.

However, the Juárez Cartel suffered a major setback with the capture of top lieutenant José Antonio Acosta Hernández, aka *El Diego*, who admitted ordering 1,500

José Antonio Acosta Hernández, aka El Diego, admitted ordering 1,500 killings, including the massacre of 16 students at a high school party in Villas de Salvárcar

killings as well as conspiracy and racketeering. He was responsible for the gunning down of United States consulate employee Leslie Ann Enriquez and her husband Arthur Redelfs, along with the husband of another consulate employee, Alberto Salcido Ceniceros, as they left a children's party. He also confessed to ordering his men to kill the members of a rival gang at a January 2010 birthday party in Ciudad Juárez, which claimed the lives of sixteen, and to directing a car bombing that killed four, including two Mexican police officers. Extradited to the United States, the 34-year-old was sentenced to seven concurrent life terms and three additional consecutive life terms, plus twenty years in federal prison.

As the murder rate in Ciudad Juárez further declined, observers concluded that the New Juárez Cartel was losing ground to the *Gente Nueva*, the Sinaloa Cartel's armed wing.

House of Death

In an effort to catch Vicente Fuentes and Vicente Carrillo Leyva, US Immigration and Customs Enforcement (ICE), part of the US Department of Homeland Security, infiltrated the Juárez Cartel with an informant named Guillermo 'Lalo' Ramirez Peyro. They paid the former policeman nearly $250,000. He fingered a United States immigration official who was taking bribes and helped crack a cigarette smuggling ring, but he also continued drug smuggling on the side. When he was caught at a Border Patrol checkpoint with 100 lbs (45 kg) of marijuana stuffed into the wheels of his pick-up, he was blacklisted by the DEA, but ICE kept him on the payroll. They even worked with the federal prosecutor to get the drug charges dropped.

ICE's principal target was Heriberto 'The Engineer' Santillán Tabares, third in command of the Juárez Cartel. In August 2003, Santillán Tabares and a band of crooked Mexican police officers went on an eight-month crime spree – kidnapping, torturing and killing drug rivals in Juárez. Lalo bought duct tape to truss the victims and quicklime to dissolve the bodies. He also secretly recorded the murder of the first victim, Mexican lawyer Fernando Reyes. And he admitted that he held the victim's legs while the man was being brutally strangled, suffocated and beaten with a shovel.

'It just made me sick,' said his handler when he heard the tape. 'I had to go to the restroom and throw up. I took the recording and I told my supervisor that I didn't wish to be part of the case.'

An unknown woman shows Mexican federal agents a photo of a missing relative outside the house of Heriberto 'The Engineer' Tabares, third in command of the Juárez Cartel

Their informant had participated in first-degree murder and they should have closed the operation down. However, the United States Department of Justice was eager to proceed.

The majority of the murders took place in a house at 3633 Calle Parsonieros in a residential area of Juárez. This became known as the House of Death. Lalo's bosses told him when they were planning fresh murders, saying they were going to have a 'barbecue' and he was to prepare the place. He was present at several killings and admitted driving two victims to the house, knowing that they were going to be killed.

On 15 January 2004, Lalo lured Santillán Tabares to El Paso, where he was arrested and eventually charged with trafficking and five homicides – including that of Fernando Reyes. It was only then that the US investigators told the Mexican authorities about the House of Death. The Mexican Federal Agency of Investigations began to excavate the back garden at 3633 Calle Parsonieros after two bodies were found there.

Lalo was arrested in the United States and threatened with deportation. However, he was freed in July 2012 when the Justice Department's immigration board ruled that he might be tortured and killed if he was returned to Mexico.

THE BELTRÁN-LEYVA CARTEL

The Beltrán Leyva brothers – Marcos Arturo, Héctor, Alfredo and Carlos – were born and brought up in Badiraguato, Sinaloa. They teamed up with another boy from Badiraguato, Joaquín 'El Chapo' Guzmán Loera, and began smuggling drugs for the Sinaloa Cartel. For years they controlled the *plaza* between Tijuana and Ciudad Juárez. They also acted as a security wing for *El Chapo*, protecting his lieutenants and their families and overseeing squads of *sicarios* – assassins.

The Beltrán Leyvas remained in constant contact with *El Chapo* while he was in jail and may have helped orchestrate his escape. Arturo Beltrán Leyva, aka *El Barbas* – 'The Beard' – was with *El Chapo*, *El Mayo* and *El Azul* when they met at Monterrey and decided to take on the Tijuana Cartel, the Carrillo Fuentes family and *Los Zetas*. It is thought that he also lent a hand in the assassination of Rodolfo 'Golden Child' Carrillo Fuentes.

After Osiel Cárdenas Guillén was arrested in 2003,

Nuevo León state police were called in after two men entered a bar called La Paloma in Monterrey with assault rifles, killing the owner and wounding three other people. A few blocks away, there was a co-ordinated attack on the Rooster Bar

Carlos Beltrán Leyva kept the lowest profile of the four brothers, but his arrest in 2009 was seen by the Mexican government as evidence of the increasing effectiveness of their measures against the cartels

Arturo led the assault on the Gulf Cartel and Alfredo '*El Mochomo*' was said to have been in charge of two gangs of assassins – *Los Güeros* in Sonora and *Los Pelones* in Guerrero. However, the Beltrán Leyvas wanted to open their own *plaza* in Central Mexico, independent of Guzmán Loera, so they had a meeting with *Los Zetas* in Veracruz to discuss an alliance. This suited *Los Zetas*, who were offering their services as hit men to anyone who would oppose the Sinaloa Cartel, with the aim of building a super-cartel to challenge *El Chapo*.

Guzmán Loera got to hear of the meeting and decided to get rid of the Beltrán Leyvas, or 'cut off that arm of the organization' as he put it. A month after the meeting, Alfredo Beltrán Leyva was arrested at a house in Culiacán, together with three of his bodyguards. The police found eleven expensive watches, a luxury SUV and two suitcases stuffed with $900,000. Two other houses in Mexico City were raided and eight men were taken, along with the necessary equipment to build a drugs laboratory. There were also fragmentation grenades, assault rifles and other weapons and forty bullet-proof vests bearing the initials FEDA – said to be a Spanish acronym for 'Arturo's Special Forces'. It was thought that the men were part of three cartel 'commando' groups that were preparing attacks in response to a federal crackdown on drug traffickers.

While the authorities were glorying in having nabbed one of Guzmán Loera's former associates, the Beltrán Leyva brothers were convinced that *El Chapo* had delivered Alfredo to the authorities. Arturo Beltrán Leyva avenged himself on several senior government officials, including a federal police commissioner, and also had Guzmán Loera's son Édgar killed. But that was not all. Having provided the bodyguards for *El Chapo*'s lieutenants, the Beltrán Leyvas knew where they lived. The result was some of the worst bloodletting seen in Sinaloa.

The Beltrán Leyvas now set up on their own, with Arturo calling himself *El Jefe de Jefes* – 'The Boss of Bosses'. But without Guzmán Loera, the Beltrán Leyva brothers no longer enjoyed political protection. Alfredo had allegedly been paying Noé Ramírez Mandujano, head of the SIEDO, $450,000 'in exchange for providing information about investigations and ongoing actions', but Ramírez Mandujano quit in July 2008 and was arrested a few months later.

Government Offensive

In December 2009 the government began an offensive against the Beltrán-Leyva Organization. On December 11 a unit of naval Special Forces backed by attack helicopters raided a house in a luxury gated community in the town of Tepoztlán, Morelos, 20 miles (32 km) south of Mexico City, where Arturo Beltrán Leyva was having a Christmas party. The Grammy Award-winning 'King of the Accordion' Ramón Ayala and the popular band Los Cadetes de Linares, along with twenty-four prostitutes, were hired to provide entertainment. There was a shoot out and three gunmen died, but Arturo Beltrán Leyva escaped. The military seized sixteen automatic rifles and $280,000 in cash.

Arturo Beltrán Leyva had nearly been caught before. On 7 May 2008 he was driving down the Autostrada del Sole from Guerrero, escorted by four vehicles carrying heavily armed men, when the federal police ordered him to stop. His convoy accelerated and turned off towards the town of Xoxocotla in the state of Morelos, where he was thought to have numerous hideouts. Once in Xoxocotla, two vehicles stopped, blocking the road, and there was a shoot out. One gunman was killed and a policeman died later in hospital from his wounds. Two other gunmen were arrested, but Beltrán Leyva escaped. A few hours later, the regional federal police commissioner was killed at his home.

But Arturo did not get far after the party. Using information given by the guests, Mexican naval intelligence tracked him to a luxury condominium not far away in Ahuatepec, a suburb of Cuernavaca, the capital of the state of Morelos. It was just 500 metres from the home of the governor of Morelos. Around two hundred marines stormed the condominium and searched the apartments, herding the occupants into the gym.

LEFT *Mexico City was seen as 'neutral territory' by the cartels and spared much violence. But a splinter group from the Beltrán-Leyva Cartel, Mano con Ojos (Hand with Eyes), now threatens the peace*

BELOW *Grammy Award-winner Rámon Ayala, 'King of the Accordion', was hired for Arturo Beltrán-Leyva's Christmas party which ended in a shoot out and the death of three gunmen*

Beltrán Leyva's men counterattacked, throwing grenades at the navy helicopters. Other gunmen attacked a van bringing in government reinforcements. But as night fell, the marines closed in. Arturo Beltrán Leyva phoned his old friend Édgar Valdéz Villarreal, asking for a team of hit men to help him break out. Valdéz Villarreal said that the situation was hopeless and Arturo should give himself up. Beltrán Leyva replied that he would never go peacefully.

He and his band of desperados fired back out of the windows and lobbed grenades. After two hours, the marines stormed the apartment, blowing everything apart. Arturo Beltrán Leyva was killed. His body was found covered in blood-soaked dollar bills, with his trousers around his ankles, and within hours the images were all over the internet. Three of his bodyguards also lost their lives; a fourth committed suicide.

On the other side, 30-year-old Ensign Melquisedet Angulo Córdova died and three other marines were injured. Córdova was buried with full military honours in his home town of Paraíso in Tabasco. Only hours after the funeral, gunmen burst into the family home and loosed off over thirty rounds, killing his mother, brother and aunt. A gunman named Gudiel Ivan Sanchez was later arrested in the southern state of Chiapas in connection with the crime.

BELOW *The bullet-spattered apartment where Arturo Beltrán Leyva met his end. His body was found covered in blood-soaked dollar bills. Within hours the images were all over the internet*

RIGHT *Soldiers patrol the complex in Cuernavaca after the shoot out. One marine was killed and buried with full military honours. Hours after the funeral, gunmen killed his mother, brother and aunt*

A warrant was then put out for the arrest of Carlos Beltrán Leyva. He was captured on 30 December 2009, when his car was stopped in Culiacán, Sinaloa. His driving licence, in the name of Carlos Gámes Orpineda, soon showed up as a fake. He was carrying a pistol, a rifle, ammunition, several mobile phones and packages of powder that appeared to be cocaine. The authorities held him on drug trafficking, criminal conspiracy, money laundering and firearms charges.

Héctor Beltrán Leyva took over. He was already wanted under indictments in the District of Columbia and the Eastern District of New York, and the United States had put a $5 million bounty on his head.

In league with *Los Zetas*, the Beltrán-Leyva Cartel began a violent turf war against the Gulf, Sinaloa and *La Familia* Cartels in the border city of Reynosa, Tamaulipas. By February 2010, more than sixteen people lay dead and eleven had been injured along what was known as the 'Little Border' between Reynosa and Matamoros. On the 24th, the United States Consulate in Matamoros issued a travel advisory for United States citizens in and around Reynosa, and the consulate in Reynosa was closed. The police chief of Brownsville advised United States residents not to cross the border.

In the border towns, parents kept their children out of school. The panic spread to Ciudad Victoria, capital of Tamaulipas. Senator José Julián Sacramento said: 'War has broken out in Tamaulipas.'

Break-up into Factions

Édgar Valdéz Villarreal was annoyed by the elevation of Héctor Beltrán Leyva to *El Jefe de Jefes*, a position he wanted for himself. He and his gang of assassins, Los Negros, broke away, leaving a rump that called itself *Cartel Pacifico Sur* – 'South Pacific Cartel'. In the ensuing battle, four decapitated bodies were found hanging from a bridge in Cuernavaca in August 2010 with a message saying: 'This is what will happen to all those who support the traitor Édgar Váldez Villarreal.' Soon after, Váldez Villarreal was arrested. Later he was extradited to the United States to face drugs charges.

After the departure of Váldez Villarreal, the Beltrán-Leyva Cartel broke up into small factions. The largest was *Los Mazatlecos*, from Mazatlán on the southern coast of Sinaloa. Their influence extended into the state of Nayarit to the south.

The gang's leader was Fausto Isidro Meza Flores, aka *El Chapo Isidro*, who had learned his craft with the Juárez Cartel. When Amado Carrillo Fuentes died, he went to work for the Beltrán Leyvas. Since 2008, *Los Mazatlecos* have been fighting for control of Mexico's 'Golden Triangle' states of Chihuahua, Durango and Sinaloa, where the drugs are produced.

When one of the Mazatlecos lieutenants, Geovany Lizarraga Ontiveros, was arrested in Los Mochis in May 2011 the gang attempted a daring rescue but were repelled by elements of the military.

A gift bag and accompanying narcomanta (propaganda message) at a crime scene in Cuernavaca: inside the bag was a severed head delivered with sadistic relish by the Sinaloa Cartel

They were thought to have been behind the murder of Francisco 'Pancho' Arce Rubio, leader of *Los Ántrax* who were enforcers for the Sinaloa Cartel. On 31 October 2011 gunmen went into the Deportivo Jimmy Ruiz stadium in Culiacán where Arce Rubio was playing soccer. They forced all the players to lie down on the field, then they killed one of the teams' managers, before executing Arce Rubio.

Eager for revenge, some fifty trucks belonging to *Los Ántrax* went after Isidro and the Mazatlecos, who did not back down. At least twenty died in the onslaught and *Los Mazatlecos* earned themselves the nickname 'The Nightmare of *Los Ántrax*'.

The Mazatlecos also played a major role in the shoot out at the border town of Tubutama, Sonora. The Sinaloa Cartel sent Felix the Ice Cream Man, Raúl Sabori, Paéz Soto, Nini Beltrán and *Los Jabalí*, Jose Vásquez's men,

to take out a man known only as *El Gilo* and close the Beltrán Leyva's last transit route through Sonora. They rode in a convoy of thirty or forty vehicles, all marked with the letter X on the windows. There were thought to be upwards of a hundred Sinaloa gunmen.

As the convoy approached a narrow pass, the Mazatlecos closed off the side roads and unloaded their arsenal. The vehicles were riddled with bullets. Some were killed where they sat. Others made it a few feet from their trucks before they were gunned down. At least twenty-nine died.

The Mazatlecos also gunned down Sinaloa lieutenant King Castro and singer Sergio Vega, aka *El Shaka*, was shot on the way to a gig, shortly after joking on the radio about surviving another assassination attempt. Numerous Mexican singers have been shot. They also ambushed a group of judicial police, leaving seven dead. Another forty died when the Mazatlecos joined forces

Ignacio Paéz Soto, right-hand man of El Chapo, is paraded before the press after being caught red-handed in 2009 with an AK-47, a Colt revolver and 6.6 lbs (3 kg) of cocaine. The helicopter was used to monitor the movements of his Jeep Grand Cherokee

Singer Sergio Vega, aka El Shaka, *was shot on the way to a gig shortly after he made a joke about surviving another assassination attempt*

with *Los Zetas* to take on the military. It was even reported that they had downed a helicopter. But while they made a practice of luring elite government forces into traps, their main target was *El Chapo*.

Another Beltrán Leyva splinter group, the Independent Cartel of Acapulco or CIDA, took on *La Barredora* – 'The Road Sweeper' – in Guerrero. *La Barredora*, who were also allied to the Beltrán Leyvas, developed links with the Sinaloa Cartel, while the CIDA mainly comprised members loyal to Váldez Villarreal. *Los Rojos* – 'The Reds'– also operated in Guerrero, while *Los Pelones* – 'The Bald Ones' – took over in Morelos and formed an alliance with the Gulf Cartel.

One Week in Mexico's Drug Wars

• •

TUESDAY 24 JANUARY 2012

- Two municipal police officers travelling to a police station in Ciudad Juárez, Chihuahua, killed by gunmen. Forty-eight spent shell casings from 9 mm and .223 calibre weapons found at the scene.
- Police patrol vehicle stopped in Tezonapa, Veracruz state. Two police officers forced out of the vehicle and beaten. Their vehicle torched before their assailants flee.
- Federal police engage four gunmen in a firefight outside a bar in Guadalupe, Zacatecas. Two gunmen killed in the confrontation; the other two die while trying to escape in a vehicle.
- Mexican military seize 2,085 lbs (946 kg) of marijuana being carried in a large black SUV in Sonoyta, Sonora, after its occupants abandon the vehicle and take flight.
- Mexican Army seize drug laboratory near Culiacán, Sinaloa, netting 243 gallons (921 litres) of liquid methamphetamine, approximately equivalent to 1,000 lbs (460 kg) of solid methamphetamine, and 355 lbs (161 kg) of solid methamphetamine, ready prepared, along with the following ingredients: 617 lbs (280 kg) of phenyl acetic acid; 15,979 lbs (7,248 kg) of caustic soda; 2,821 lbs (1,280 kg) of tartaric acid; 573 lbs (260 kg) of sodium acetate; and 22 lbs (10 kg) of mercury chloride. This amount of tartaric acid, applied during the final stages of meth production, is capable of producing about 1,420 lbs (640 kg) of methamphetamine. No arrests are made.

WEDNESDAY 25 JANUARY 2012

- *Narcomantas* issued by the New Juárez Cartel and addressed to Ciudad Juárez police chief Julián Leyzaola appear in at least ten separate places around Ciudad Juárez, Chihuahua. The messages

Part of a clandestine drug-processing lab found in a mangrove swamp near Culiacán, 24 January 2012

warn that a police officer will be killed daily unless Leyzaola stops supporting *El Chapo* and arresting NCJ members.

- Bodies of a man and woman found near a dock in El Batamote, near Culiacán, Sinaloa. The man was decapitated, with his head placed near his feet. A message reads: 'For continuing to steal cars. AAAA.' Possibly the work of the *Artistas Asesinos*.
- Body of lawyer Daniel Jaime Nunez found in Atoyac de Alvarez, Guerrero, with a gunshot wound to the head. A note says: 'This will happen to all kidnappers, extortionists, and robbers.'
- Gunmen pull eight people out of vehicles at a street corner in Monterrey, Nuevo León, then shoot and kill them, leaving a *narcomanta* reportedly addressed to a rival gang. Authorities do not reveal the wording of the message. Ninth body found nearby, but her connection to the other victims is unknown.

THURSDAY 26 JANUARY 2012

- Gunmen open fire on the Mexican military from a vehicle in Práxedis G. Guerrero, Chihuahua state. Three gunmen detained and three assault rifles, one handgun and 289 rounds of various calibres are seized, along with 14 lbs (6.5 kg) of marijuana.

Gunmen said to belong to the *Gente Nueva*, a Sinaloa Federation enforcer group.

- Fifteen gunmen enter a bar and shoot three people at a table in Neza, Mexico State. They flee the scene before police arrive.
- Gunmen open fire on the escort travelling with Manuel Añorve Baños, the mayor of Acapulco, Guerrero, killing a police officer and a city employee. Authorities find at least twenty AK-47 shell casings at the scene.
- Gunmen drag two semi-naked women from a vehicle and shoot both in the head outside a primary school in Monterrey, Nuevo León. The women have their hands bound and their heads covered. 'Zeta' and 'Z' are written in several places on a wall behind them.
- In Zapopan, Jalisco, Mexican federal police arrest seven members of the Jalisco New Generation Cartel, including leader Abundio Mendoza Gaytan, aka *El Guero Abundis* – 'The Abundant Blond' – for kidnapping, extortion and the sale and distribution of drugs.

Police guard the body of a fellow officer who was pulled from his vehicle in Ciudad Juárez, then shot and killed

FRIDAY 27 JANUARY 2012

- Gunman in a black SUV kills two police officers travelling in an unmarked car in Ciudad Juárez, Chihuahua.
- José Luis Zea Frescas, a regional public defence co-ordinator in Ciudad Juárez, killed by unidentified gunman, shot five times with a .40-calibre weapon.
- State and municipal police arrest 204 individuals at La Eternidad bar in Monterrey, Nuevo León state, in connection with the January 25 execution of eight people at a street corner and three women found nearby. The victims of the shooting were last seen at the bar. La Eternidad is near El Sabino Gordo, a bar where gunmen murdered twenty people on 8 July 2011.
- Two gunmen kill a woman as she is leaving her house for work in Ciudad Juárez, Chihuahua state. They engage her in conversation before shooting her at least twice.

SATURDAY 28 JANUARY 2012

- Dismembered body of an employee at a criminal court in Guerrero state found in the boot of a car along with a *narcomanta* warning that a similar

fate awaits anyone who supports Victor Aguirre, the Undersecretary of Public Safety, and prison director Antelmo Rodríguez Salgado. The message is signed 'El Chapo'.

- Three bodies found on a soccer field in Ciudad Juárez. They were handcuffed and gagged before being executed.
- A municipal police officer is pulled out of his vehicle in Ciudad Juárez, then shot and killed. He was driving his private car home after leaving work. The murder brings the number of municipal police officers killed in Ciudad Juárez in January 2012 to eleven.
- Gunmen attack a military vehicle in Cadereyta, Nuevo León. Two gunmen are killed during the firefight.
- Seven bodies are found in a clandestine grave in Ejutla, Jalisco. Four have been burned; three are decomposing.
- Gunmen enter a house in Tijuana, Baja California. They order the women to lie on the floor and take the five male occupants to the kitchen, where they are shot. The brother of one of the victims was a former municipal police officer who was head of security for Alfredo Arteaga Gonzalez – aka El Aquiles, 'The Talons' – a Sinaloa Cartel operator in Baja California.
- Mexican authorities arrest Roberto López 'El Chato' Virgen, a leader of the Jalisco New Generation Cartel in Colima. He was injured during a shoot out prior to his arrest.

SUNDAY 29 JANUARY 2012

- Prison riot at the Aquiles Serdan prison in Chihuahua kills four inmates and injures at least seven others. It began with a gang fight between Los Aztecas and Los Mexicles, who used makeshift weapons.
- Three are arrested in Acapulco, Guerrero, carrying the remains of a dismembered body in their vehicle, along with nine narcomantas, including those by the Gente Nueva and El Chapo Comando Del Diablo. They attempted to escape and engaged in a firefight, though no one was injured in the exchange.

MONDAY 30 JANUARY 2012

- A man's body, with hands and feet bound, is found in front of his home in Ciudad Juárez, after a visit by unidentified callers. Neighbours say he was involved in the drugs trade.
- Arrest of Enrique Elizondo 'El Arabe' Flores, aka El Cuervo – 'The Crow' – an operator in Nuevo León. Elizondo confesses to seventy-five murders.
- Gunmen travelling in six vehicles ambush municipal police in Ciudad Juárez while the officers are filling up their vehicles at a petrol station. Three gunmen are killed and three police officers are wounded.

Enrique Elizondo 'El Arabe' Flores, aka El Cuervo (The Crow), who videotaped himself dancing to reggae music in the street as he cut off the fingers of victims

Spectral army: Mexican troops seem to be consumed by fire as they supervise the burning of several tons of seized drugs which, without their intervention, would have been destined to fan the flames of drug misery in the US

LA FAMILIA CARTEL

La Familia Michoacana had its origins in an outfit called *La Empresa* – 'The Business'– which was formed in 1985 by Carlos Alberto Rosales Mendoza. Other early leaders were Nazario Moreno González, known as *El Más Loco* – 'The Craziest One' – and José de Jesús Méndez Vargas, aka *El Chango* – 'The Monkey'. Moreno González claimed that *La Familia* began as a vigilante group to fight the Milenio Cartel, an offshoot of the Sinaloas run by the Valencia brothers in the state of Michoacán.

But *La Familia* did not have the resources to overcome the Milenio Cartel, so they found it necessary to ask Osiel Cárdenas Guillén to send the Zetas to help. Two of the Zetas' deadliest elements, Efraín Teodoro 'El Efra' Torres – Z-14 – and Gustavo González Castro, aka *El Erótico* – 'The Erotic One' – were dispatched at the head of a gang of *sicarios* to do the job.

Rosales Mendoza was arrested in 2004 while preparing to bust Cárdenas Guillén out of prison. *Los Zetas* then sought to take over the lucrative *plazas* in Guerrero and Michoacán. They had in their sights Lázaro Cárdenas, the principal port of Michoacán. *La*

Familia were not happy with this, so Moreno González, Méndez Vargas and their twelve top followers known as 'The Apostles' decided to fight.

They adopted Special Forces techniques with hit-and-run ambushes, PsyOps – psychological warfare – *narcomantas*, taunting press releases, threatening notes left on corpses and gruesome videos uploaded to YouTube. After beheading victims and mutilating their corpses, they castrated them and shoved their genitals in their mouths.

The most notorious beheading incident occurred in Uruapan. Late at night on 6 September 2006, armed men in military garb stormed the Sol y Sombra bar and emptied out a heavy plastic bag. Five severed heads rolled across the dance floor. The gunman left a note that read: '*La Familia* doesn't kill for money, kill women, or kill innocents. Only those who deserve to die will die. Let everyone know that this is divine justice.'

'This is not something you see every day,' said a bartender, who would not give his name for fear of losing his own head.

Forty-four members of La Familia *arrive for an unscheduled stop in Mexico City after being arrested in April 2009. Their ideology featured a mix of evangelical self-help notions and insurgent peasant slogans*

The day before, the killers had kidnapped the five victims from a car repair shop, where they had been selling crystal meth. Their heads were sawn off with a bowie knife while they were still alive.

War on the Police

At that time, a war was being waged against the police, who were systematically terrorized. That February, Commander Gonzalo Domínguez Díaz, a state policeman in Pátzcuaro, arrested two men on weapons charges. Minutes later he received death threats from a local businessman who had connections to the cartels. The case was then thrown out for lack of evidence.

Later in the year, he heard on the street that gunmen were looking for him. He told his wife that if he arrested them he would be risking his life, particularly as the courts would probably let them go. On 8 May, he was driving home at around 6.30 pm when a car pulled in front of him. He was shot once in the head with a 12-gauge shotgun at point blank range and twice in the chest with an AK-47. It was over so fast that he never even had a chance to draw his sidearm.

Then in August the second-in-command of the state

Fanny Carranza Domínguez holds up the bloodied shirt worn by her husband, the state police commander in Pátzcuaro, Michoacán, who was gunned down after prosecutors released some gangsters he had arrested

police in Uruapan was murdered. Walking to his car at 3:30 one afternoon, he was just a hundred yards from police headquarters when he was surrounded by fifteen heavily armed men in black commando outfits, like those worn by federal agents. They hustled him into a waiting vehicle and sped off. His body was found the next day at a nearby ranch. He had been shot twenty-five times. With the body was a note that read: 'For playing with two bands.'

As well as attacking the suppliers of ice – crystal meth – *La Familia* fought for control of the marijuana and poppy fields, the processing plants and the transit routes. They also branched out into human trafficking, smuggling, extortion, kidnapping, loan-sharking and the local sales of marijuana and cocaine.

In the summer of 2008, Zeta Alfredo Rangel Buendia, aka *El Chicles* – 'The Chewing Gum' – was arrested. He admitted that one of his missions was to assassinate *La Familia*'s *El Chango* and *El Más Loco*. But it seemed *Los Zetas* were losing the battle. *La Familia*'s Francisco Javier Torres Mora, aka *El Camello*, spent his time kidnapping *Los Zetas* members and men from the Beltrán-Leyva Cartel. Meanwhile *narcomantas* went up in Michoacán and Guerrero, warning the Zetas to leave or die. They stressed that *La Familia* considered that they were fighting *bestias del mal* – 'evil beasts'. *La Familia Michoacana* promised to become the Guanajuato family in Guanajuato, as well as the Guerrero family in Guerrero.

But while the Mexican armed forces captured five Zetas and a cache of arms in Valle de Santiago, 50 miles (80 km) south of Guanajuato's state capital, in February 2010, five decapitated bodies were found near Apatzingán, Michoacán, a *La Familia* stronghold. Two of the torsos had the letter 'Z' carved on their backs and a note which read: 'You're next dude and all the *Familia* dogs… Greetings Frey, Sincerely *Los Z.*'

During the next two weeks' fighting between *La Familia* and *Los Zetas*, there were twenty-one beheadings. On 10 February 2010, three victims were not just decapitated but were completely dismembered. Again their body parts had the letter 'Z' carved on them before they were tossed in black garbage bags and dumped in downtown Morelia. By the end of March, there were seventy-seven such mutilated corpses.

Moral High Ground

La Familia continued to assume the moral high ground. In 2010, in Zamora, six alleged criminals were whipped with barbed wire and boards. They were then forced to parade around the streets carrying signs that said: 'I am a rat and *La Familia* is punishing me' and 'This is for all delinquents. *La Familia* is here, citizens. Don't judge us. We are cleaning your city.'

Proceso magazine maintained that the members of *La Familia* were regular churchgoers who carried Bibles and distributed them around government offices. They justified killings by saying they were following an 'order from the Lord'; they ran rehab centres, which gave them ready access to recruits; they campaigned against the use of drugs and alcohol and demanded respect for women; they administered the organization *Jóvenes: Arte y Cultura* – 'Youth: Art and Culture' – to lure more youngsters into their ranks; and they held month-long induction courses, reportedly employing the works of American Christian motivational speaker John Eldredge.

Although Eldredge does not espouse violence, *La Familia* had no such qualms. Captured *La Familia* member Miguel 'El Tyson' Ortiz Miranda described the training of *La Familia*'s hit men. They were taken to Jesús del Monte in the mountains, where they hunted victims and then shot and cooked them. This was to test recruits and teach them to overcome fear and any squeamishness they might harbour about the sight of blood. He did not say whether they ate their victims. However, this would not be unusual. Arturo Beltrán Leyva would serve unsuspecting dinner guests meat sliced from his victims, in a spicy sauce.

Ortiz Miranda himself was linked to the murder of twelve federal police officers in Zitácuaro and four other officers on the highway to Tarimbaro. A former police officer, he confessed to the murder of Michoacán's public safety secretary José Manuel Revuelta and Josafat Delfino López Tinoco, director of investigations for the Federal Attorney General's Office.

Political Influence

La Familia also exercised considerable political influence. In November 2007, mayoral candidates in Múgica and Nueva Italia stepped down after receiving death threats. Elsewhere the electorate were dissuaded from voting for those standing against *La Familia*'s favoured candidates. In 2009, the cartel also gave its backing to certain candidates standing for the Chamber of Deputies.

Those who opposed *La Familia* could expect no mercy. In April 2009, the body of Nicolás León Hernández, twice municipal president of Lázaro Cárdenas, was found. He had been tortured and shot dead. An accompanying note read: 'This is for all who support *Los Zetas*. Sincerely, F.M.' – *Familia Michoacana*.

They have also extended their influence into Mexico City, Mexico State, Jalisco, Guanajuato and Nayarit – key staging posts along the drug routes that ran from Colombia through Venezuela, Panama and Guatemala and on to cells in Dallas, Houston, Atlanta, California and North Carolina.

After arrests in May 2009, a witness said that favoured mayoral candidates were given 2 million pesos – $155,000 – and 200,000 pesos – $15,500 – a month if they won. He also said that Leonel Godoy Rangel, governor of Michoacán from 2008 to 2012, received $300,000 from each of *La Familia*'s leaders – a charge he strenuously denied. So many of *La Familia*'s favoured candidates won in the 2011 elections that it was called a *narco-elección*.

The money *La Familia* spends on politicians is a drop in the ocean compared to the amount it makes from crystal meth, despite its public condemnation of the drug. One laboratory operator said that it cost a million pesos – $77,000 – to set up a lab that would then produce 220 lbs (100 kg) of ice, worth 3.5 million pesos – $270,000 – a week. In 2010, federal forces closed down forty labs, many of which were around Apatzingán, Michoacán in the

The Milenio Cartel

The Milenio Cartel began operations in 1997 as *Los Valencia*, a gang operating under the umbrella of the Sinaloa Cartel headed by the Valencia brothers – Armando, Luis, Juan and Ventura. Through Guillermo Moreno Ríos – who was indicted for drug trafficking alongside Armando 'Juanito' Valencia Cornelio in 1999 – they had good connections in Colombia. Armando Valencia had previously lived in Anaheim, California, where he had met Nemesio '*El Mencho*' Oseguera Cervantes, who became the cartel's chief of *sicarios* and later a leader of the Jalisco New Generation Cartel.

Having bought an avocado plantation in Michoacán, they began importing cocaine from Colombia in co-operation with Sinaloans in Jalisco, Nayarit and Colima. In October 1999, Moreno Ríos, then the cartel's chief of operations in Zapopan, a suburb of Guadalajara, was arrested along with three Colombians and an American. Nevertheless, the Milenio Cartel went on to supply one third of the cocaine consumed in the United States in the first decade of the 21st century, focusing its trade on California, Texas, New York and Chicago.

In 2003, Armando Valencia was arrested and

sentenced to forty-seven years in jail. Four years later, Ventura was gunned down in Tepalcatepec. A message nailed to his chest taunted his brothers and was signed '*Mencho*'. His skull had caved in under his attackers' blows and a dead dog had been left at his feet.

When *Los Zetas* moved into Michoacán, drug-related killings soared from a few dozen in 2000 to 543 in 2006. The federal authorities tried to crack down with Joint Operation Michoacán. In December 2006, four of the Milenio Cartel's top lieutenants were arrested.

By then the cartel had gone into the production of crystal meth with laboratories hidden in the hills around Apatzingán. The precursor chemicals were thought to have been provided by a shadowy Mexican-Chinese named Zhenli Ye Gon.

Oscar Nava Valencia, aka *El Lobo* – 'The Wolf' – was arrested after a gun battle with the army in Tlajomulco de Zuñiga, a small town near Guadalajara, in October 2009. The last brother, Juan Nava Valencia, was arrested in Guadalajara in May 2010. What remained of the Milenio Cartel moved to Guadalajara, where they formed an alliance with *Los Zetas*.

Sitting pretty in this police line-up is Oscar Nava Valencia, aka 'The Wolf'. He was arrested after a gun battle with the army near Guadalajara in October 2009

Sierra Madre, where there were poppy and marijuana fields and small landing strips.

When President Calderón came to power he visited Apatzingán wearing the uniform of commander-in-chief of the army to inaugurate 'Operation Michoacán', which had claimed the lives of sixty soldiers, a hundred police officers and five hundred cartel gunmen.

Calderón also went after the politicians who allowed *La Familia* to operate with impunity. Michoacán's Secretary of Public Security, Citallí Fernández González, was forced to step down for her failure to curtail drug trafficking. She was arrested in the round-up of 27 May 2009 that culled thirty-two public officials, including twelve mayors. One of them was Uriel Farías Álvarez, aka *El Paisa* – 'The Confidant'. He was the brother of Juan José Farías Álvarez, aka *El Abuelo* – 'The Godfather' – a leader of the Milenio Cartel who was thought to have been behind the killing of members of *Los Zetas* and *La Familia* throughout Michoacán in 2006. Before his 2007 landslide election victory in Tepalcatepec, a key staging post on the border between Michoacán and Jalisco, Uriel Farías Álvarez told the electorate: 'My brother only kept lookout on the orders of the army. And as a result they said he was a *narco*.'

The opposition, led by Leonel Godoy Rangel, condemned the arrest of politicians.

In 2009 Godoy's brother, Julio César Godoy Toscano, won a federal congressional seat for Lázaro Cárdena, but before he took office he was indicted for money laundering and having ties to organized crime. Once he became a congressman he would have immunity, so he evaded arrest by sneaking into his swearing-in ceremony.

When a recording of him accepting a bribe of twenty-five million pesos – $2 million – from Servando '*La Tuta*' Gómez Martínez, a lieutenant of *La Familia*, was released, congress voted to revoke his immunity. He then disappeared and Mexico's attorney general asked Interpol for help in catching him.

La Familia organized a convoy of buses to carry protesters to Mexico City to demonstrate against the arrest of Uruapan's mayor.

'I'm just here because *La Familia* told me to come,' one protester told the *Observer*. 'I know they are really crazy. In fact, I think they are sick sometimes, but they

Six members of La Familia *are brought to book. If you wanted promotion within the cartel, you had to attend church as well as practise your shooting skills. Their leaders considered themselves idealists, but most of them had blood on their hands*

are the only people in my town who can help you out if you get in trouble, so that's why I joined the group.'

Reacting to the protests, the Secretary of the Interior Fernando Gómez Mont addressed *La Familia* directly.

'We are ready for you,' he said. 'Deal with authority and not with citizens. We are waiting. This is an invitation to you.'

Other politicians condemned this bravado and by and large the arrested officials were released due to lack of evidence.

Leonel Godoy Rangel was still complaining about President Calderón sending the army into his state without informing him first when another federal incursion into Michoacán netted Wenceslao '*El Wencho*'

Álvarez Álvarez, an ally of *La Familia* in Nueva Italia. He claimed that he had been a legitimate farmer until the kidnap and murder of his father made him side with the narco-traffickers, though he denied trafficking himself.

According to the attorney general's office, his cocaine network ran from Colombia to Guatemala, Honduras, El Salvador, Venezuela and the Dominican Republic, and then on through Mexico to Atlanta and other United States cities. The DEA linked him to Rosales Mendoza and El-40, number two in *Los Zetas*. He was also said to have laundered millions of dollars through Monterrey, Nuevo Laredo and Atlanta. Álvarez Álvarez maintained that he and his family made their money by growing tomatoes, peppers and mangos.

La Familia's Mission

Unlike other cartels *La Familia* issued a manifesto, which was printed as a newspaper advertisement in November 2006. It read:

The Michoacán Family

WHO ARE WE?
Ordinary workers from the hot lands of Michoacán, united by the need to end the oppression and humiliation which we have been subjected to by the people perpetually in power, which allowed them to perpetrate all kinds of dirty tricks and abuses through the state. These include members of the Milenio Cartel... and those who have carried out kidnappings, extortions, and other crimes that disturb the peace in Michoacán.

OUR MISSION:
To eradicate from the state of Michoacán kidnapping, extortion, assassinations, hijackings, theft of vehicle, and burglaries perpetrated by the people mentioned who have made the state of Michoacán an unsafe place. Our only motive is that we love our state and can no longer stand by to see the people's dignity trampled under foot... It is possible to ward off these delinquents who come from other states. We will not allow them to enter Michoacán and continue committing crimes.

We are eradicating completely the sale of the lethal drug crystal meth, which causes irreversible damage to society. We will also prohibit the sale of altered wine from Tepito.

OUR OBJECTIVE:
To maintain the universal values and rights of the people. But to eradicate these ills, we have had to use tough tactics, as it is the only way to bring order to the state. We will not let it get out of control again.

WHY DID WE FORM?
When the *Familia Michoacana* began, we did not think we could get rid of kidnapping, assassination, fraud, and the sale of crystal meth. But many people have faith and we are succeeding.

La Familia has grown until it has covered the whole of Michoacán. It sprang from a commitment to combat crime that was out of control in our state. *La Familia* has made advances little by little, but we cannot claim victory yet. However we can say that there has been an eighty per cent improvement in these problems and we have reduced kidnapping by the same percentage. People who work in any decent occupation need not fear. We respect them...

When we first proposed ending to the sale of the crystal meth, many told us that not even First World countries have been able to do this. Nevertheless, we are managing to do it.

FOR THOUGHT:
As a resident of Michoacán, what would you do? Would you join *La Familia* if you saw that we are fighting these crimes? Or would you let them proliferate?

Family man, do you like seeing your son out on the streets where he is in danger of getting involved in drugs or crime? Or would you support an organization that fights these maladies?

The media have been responsible and objective in their coverage of events and we appreciate their impartiality. Other nations have not seen such organizations formed on the people's behalf, and yet we have already begun... Success depends on the support and understanding of Michoacán society.

Sincerely,
La Familia Michoacána

Project Coronado

In October 2009, the United States federal government launched Project Coronado against *La Familia*. It was to be the largest operation against a Mexican drug cartel in the United States.

Nearly four years in the planning, it was conducted in 38 cities from Boston to Seattle and led to the arrest of 1,186 suspects in 19 states and the seizure of 4,407 lbs (1,999 kg) of cocaine, 2,711 lbs (1,230 kg) of methamphetamine, 29 lbs (13 kg) of heroin, 16,389 lbs (7,434 kg) of marijuana, 389 weapons, 269 motor

vehicles and two boats, along with $32.8 million.

Naming *La Familia* specifically, FBI Director Robert S. Mueller III said: 'We have dealt a substantial blow to a group that has polluted our neighborhoods with illicit drugs and has terrorized Mexico with unimaginable violence.'

United States Attorney General Eric Holder added that the raids had 'dealt a significant blow to *La Familia*'s supply chain'.

But *La Familia* was not dead yet. Project Coronado was followed by Project Delirium, spearheaded by the Department of Justice in mid-2011. Another 221 suspected

La Familia members were arrested. Over the next twenty months, 260 lbs (118 kg) of cocaine, 635 lbs (288 kg) of methamphetamines and 24 lbs (11 kg) of heroin were seized, along with $770,499 in cash.

Deputy Attorney General James Cole told the press: 'The arrests and seizures we are announcing today have stripped *La Familia* of its manpower, its deadly product, and its profit, and helped make communities large and small safer.'

There was also internal strife within *La Familia* between the followers of *El Más Loco* and *El Chango*, who phoned Osiel Cárdenas in jail. On his mobile phone *El*

Mata Amigos told Méndez Vargas: 'Nazario is unstable; his erratic behavior jeopardizes *La Familia*. You would be wise to cast your lot with the Sinaloa and Gulf Cartels against *Los Zetas*.'

This caused a terminal split in *La Familia*.

The mining town of Angangueo is set amid picturesque landscape but susceptible to subsidence and terrible landslides. This sums up the precarious nature of life in much of Michoacán

THE KNIGHTS TEMPLAR CARTEL

In response to Osiel Cárdenas' appeal from jail, *La Familia* sent troops to join the *Fusión de Cárteles Antizeatas* (FCAZ) – 'Fusion of Anti-Zeta Cartels'. However, the Michoacán Cartel seemed to be dealt a terminal blow with the announcement of the death of Nazario '*Más Loco*' Moreno Gonzáles on 8 December 2010, after a two-day shoot out with the Mexican authorities.

Moreno Gonzáles had been the spiritual leader of *La Familia* and seems to have been the inspiration behind the Knights Templar. Styling himself the 'saviour of the people', he had seen the cartel as a guerrilla movement, rather than as a criminal organization.

LEFT *Guru of bloodshed Nazario Moreno Gonzáles was known as 'Más Loco', usually translated as 'The Craziest One'*

BELOW *A policeman emerges from the Knights Templar roadside chapel in honour of St Nazario at Buenavista, 22 May 2013*

Born on 8 March 1970, little is known about his early life. He was, however, very religious. As an adult he preached in his home town of Apatzingán, Michoacán.

Más Loco emigrated illegally to the United States as a teenager, first settling in California and then moving to Texas. There he got into the drugs trade. His first arrest for drug trafficking took place in McAllen, Texas, in 1994. Then in 2003, a federal grand jury in McAllen indicted him on charges that included conspiracy to distribute marijuana, cocaine and methamphetamine. A warrant was issued for his arrest, accusing him of six transactions that involved the importation of more than five tons of marijuana to the United States. As a result, he fled back to Mexico.

While raised a Catholic, he became a Jehovah's Witness in the United States. He was also influenced by the book *Wild At Heart*, written by the evangelical author John Eldredge of the Colorado-based Ransomed Heart Ministries. In January, a car was seized in Michoacán. In it were twenty-three guns, four grenades and nine copies of *Salvaje de Corazón* (*Wild At Heart*), with an inscription signed by 'The Craziest One'.

Moreno Gonzáles' wife hosted self-improvement seminars in Michoacán. One held in Apatzingán was promoted with posters bearing the slogan: 'Let's help create a better future'. *Más Loco* is thought to have written a book himself, sometimes known as *The Sayings of the Craziest One or The Family Bible*, outlining the religious dimensions of the cartel.

He insisted that his men eschew alcohol and drugs – which were only to be trafficked into the United States, not sold in Mexico itself. They were recruited at drug rehabilitation centres and then forced to renounce their drug-taking habit. Discipline was strict and failure to live up to the cartel's ideals was punishable by death. Women were to be treated with respect and thieves were beaten and forced to walk naked through the town, carrying placards.

The Mexican government profile said Moreno 'erected himself as the "Messiah", using the Bible to profess to poor people and obtain their loyalty'. He also vowed to keep President Calderón's home state – Michoacán – out of the hands of other cartels.

Despite his pretensions, he found himself on the United States Department of Justice's 'Kingpin Act' list. United States citizens and companies are prohibited from having any business dealings with those on the list and any assets they might have in the United States are frozen.

Acting under Moreno Gonzáles' leadership, the cartel trafficked drugs and fought a ruthless war against other cartels. It then diversified into prostitution, extortion, counterfeiting, kidnapping, armed robbery and levying protection money in lieu of taxes, laundering the money through bent car dealerships. On the other hand, Moreno Gonzáles offered loans to farmers, businesses, schools and churches, and provided support for the poor. Mexico put a bounty of 30 million pesos – $2 million – on his head.

In December 2010, Moreno Gonzáles decided to have a party in Apatzingán that was initially billed as a peace rally, where he was going to hand out Christmas presents. Some three hundred people turned up. A gunfight broke out and the police arrived to investigate. Gunmen fired on their cars and soon they were involved in an all-out firefight.

'They had look-outs so they were waiting for us. We drove into the town and there was a wall of some forty trucks and they attacked us,' said Elias Alvarez, the police commander who led the operation in Apatzingán. 'It was a very hard battle.'

Five officers and three civilians – including an eight-month-old baby and a teenage girl – were killed in the shoot out. The police also claimed to have killed fifty gunmen. In retaliation, gunmen torched vehicles across Michoacán and used them as barricades, even blockading all the roads out of the state capital of Morelia to prevent the federal police sending reinforcements.

During the firefight at Apatzingán, it was thought that Moreno Gonzáles had been gunned down, but the gunmen carried off his body so it was impossible to be sure. Afterwards people came out to demonstrate their support. One placard read: 'Nazario will always live in our hearts.' Rumours persisted, however, that *Más Loco* was still alive.

The Downfall of *La Familia*

Two of Moreno Gonzáles' acolytes – Servando '*La Tuta*' Gómez Martínez and Enrique '*El Kike*' Plancarte Solís – challenged *El Chango* Méndez Vargas for leadership of the cartel, calling their breakaway outfit *Los Caballeros Templarios* – 'The Knights Templar'.

José de Jesús Mendes, aka El Chango, *who was captured at a police checkpoint in the state of Aguascalientes. The Mexican government had put a reward of $2m on his head*

Gómez Martínez was described as the operational chief of the cartel in October 2009, when he was named in a United States Justice Department indictment for conspiring to import and distribute cocaine in the United States. The indictment said Gómez was in charge of acquiring weapons for the cartel and might be behind the murder of twelve Mexican federal law enforcement officers. Their bodies were found in July 2009, following the arrest of another *La Familia*

leader, Arnoldo Rueda Medina, aka *La Minsa*.

His second-in-command, Plancarte Solís, was in charge of the operation to produce and smuggle methamphetamine. Both have $2 million bounties on their heads.

El Chango fought back by making a pact with the Beltrán Leyvas, but they were too weak to help. The two warring mini-cartels in Jalisco – *La Resistencia* ('The Resistance') and *Cártel de Jalisco Nueva Generación* – both refused his overtures.

Through *El Wencho*, he made contact with El-40, but the authorities caught eleven Zetas on the border of Jalisco and Michoacán, on their way to lend a helping hand. Then on 21 June 2011, he was captured at a checkpoint in Aguascalientes. His men quickly defected to the Knights Templar.

The Knights Templar then added insult to injury by formally expelling Méndez Vargas from *La Familia* for making an alliance with *Los Zetas*. *Narcomantas* announced:

> '*To the Michoacana society in general. We are informing you that* La Familia Michoacana *separates itself from all acts by* Chango *Méndez and his allies who formed part of* La Familia Michoacan, *because* El Chango*'s degraded actions… have caused his expulsion because of his links to the social cancer of* Los Zetas. *We wish to make it clear that* La Familia *represents all Michoacanos not* Chango *Méndes.*'

What was left of *El Chango*'s branch of *La Familia* was taken over by Jesús *El Changito* Méndez, one of *El Chango*'s fourteen children. He was supported by his younger brother Fernando, *El Pony* Herrera Ramírez and Martín Rosales Magaña. In 2011, a shoot out between the two groups left ten dead.

On 7 August 2011, the Mexican attorney general reported that *La Familia* had been disbanded. Some members had joined the Sinaloa Cartel and some *Los Zetas*, with the bulk going to the Knights Templar.

Meanwhile the Knights Templar were handing out a twenty-two page booklet called *The Code of the Knights Templar of Michoacán*, claiming that they were battling poverty, tyranny and injustice. They said they would 'begin a challenging ideological battle to defend the values

The Code of the Knights Templar of Michoacán, a booklet which typically was handed out to bus passengers in the region and to members of the rural population

of society based on ethics'. Elsewhere they proclaimed: 'God is the truth and there is no truth without God.' Cartel members 'must fight against materialism' and not kill women and children for money.

The booklet was illustrated with pictures of the medieval Knights Templar, who fought Muslim armies for the control of Jerusalem. Curiously close to the presumed burial site of Moreno Gonzáles, a number of white crosses have appeared carrying Muslim names such as Muhammad, Abdul Azim, Sulaiman and Abu Sufian.

The Pope and the Knights Templar Cartel

During Pope Benedict XVI's visit to Mexico in March 2012, the Knights Templar Cartel declared a truce. A week before he arrived, they hung out *narcomantas* in towns across the state of Guanajuato saying: 'The Knights Templar Cartel will not partake in any warlike acts, we are not killers, welcome Pope.'

The previous month they had hung out other banners hinting that they would be calling a ceasefire. They urged the other cartels to do the same and warned them not to provoke the *Caballeros Templarios*, or Knights Templar, by moving into their territory. One read:

'We just want to warn that we do not want more groups in the state of Guanajuato. Confrontations will be inevitable. You have been warned, New Generation, we want Guanajuato in peace, so don't think about moving in and much less causing violence, precisely at this time when His Holiness Benedict XVI is coming.'

Pope Benedict smiles benignly out over a sea of faces as children release doves during his visit to Guanajuato

The move seems to have been a response to the Archbishop of León, in Guanajuato, who asked the cartels to abstain from violence while His Holiness was visiting the city. Guanajuato was a battleground for the Knights Templar and the Jalisco New Generation Cartel.

However, the Pope's visit to Mexico did not pass without incident in Michoacán, the Knights Templars' home state. On 23 March, the day the Pope arrived in the country, two federal police officers were found dead on the highway outside Morelia, Michoacán's capital. They had been shot at close range with a high-calibre weapon. These were the hallmarks of organized crime.

There were two other murders that weekend. First, the police found the body of an unidentified torture victim abandoned in the countryside. Then another killing took place during a bicycle theft that went

wrong, though other groups might well have been responsible. Elsewhere, a federal police vehicle came under fire on 24 March while out on patrol. Meanwhile crime-fighting activities continued as normal, with the military dismantling two laboratories used for the production of crystal meth, the main source of income for the Knights Templar and their rivals *La Familia Michoacana*.

The Knights Templar had been part of *La Familia* until it split off in March 2011. Then they hung banners across Michoacán state proclaiming that they would now be carrying out the 'altruistic activities that were previously performed by *La Familia Michoacana*'. This followed the death of Nazario Moreno González, who gave out 'bibles' of his sayings to his followers and was venerated as a saint. Some say that Moreno is still alive and now heads the Knights Templar.

The titular head of the Knights Templar is Moreno's number two, Servando Gómez Martínez – *La Tuta*. In a video he released in August 2012, he described the peaceful philosophy of the cartel. It was, he said, 'a brotherhood, founded by a set of statutes and codes', dedicated to protecting the people of Michoacán from organized crime, particularly the Zetas. According to its *narcomantas*, it is fighting against 'materialism, injustice and tyranny'.

While the ceasefire was not followed to the letter, it did have the effect of making the Knights Templar look like one of the more community-minded cartels. However, it followed the recent arrest of the Knights Templars' leader in Guanajuato and might have been a cynical ploy to give the leaderless group a breathing space before a new boss emerged.

Guanajuato was the birthplace of several well-known artists, including Diego Rivera and Olga Costa. Until recently it enjoyed a low crime rate

The Craziest One Lives

After the arrest of Mario Buenrostro Quiroz, alleged leader of a Mexico City-based drug gang known as 'Los Aboytes', his video-taped interrogation was released. In it he said that he had been a member of La Familia. He then claimed that Moreno Gonzáles was still alive and heading the Knights Templar. Narcomantas also proclaimed that Moreno Gonzáles was not dead. There was even talk of a 'second coming'.

Roadside shrines to 'San Nazario' have sprung up. There were reports that he had baptized people while dressed as St Francis of Assisi and he was widely thought to have appeared in Morelia after his son had been killed in a motorcycle accident. Another story has it that Moreno Gonzáles' sister turned up at the morgue to collect the body, but the coroner would not release it until there had been an autopsy. Then Moreno Gonzáles turned up and persuaded him. It was also said that the people in the car that had hit the boy's motorcycle had disappeared soon

Mexican soldiers display members of the Knights Templar arrested at a ranch not far from Morelia in 2012. Far from being crusaders, in the cold light of day they turned out to be ruthless criminals with guns and drugs

Extracts from The Code of the Knights Templar of Michoacán

- I swear and promise to always seek to protect the oppressed, the widow, and the orphan.
- The Knights of the Order must conduct themselves with humility and be the most honourable, the most noble, the most courteous, the most honest, and the most chivalrous.
- The members of the Order must fight against materialism, injustice, and tyranny in the world.
- The Knights Templar will begin a challenging ideological battle to defend the values of a society based on ethics.
- A Templar soldier cannot be enslaved by sectarian beliefs or narrow-minded opinions... a Templar must always seek the truth, because God is in the truth.
- The Order promotes patriotism and the expression of pride in one's own land.
- It is prohibited to abuse the innocence of chaste women, and minors, using power or trickery to seduce them.
- The council's authorization is required for the use of deadly force.
- A Knight who breaks the vow of silence of the Knights Templar of the state of Michoácan will receive a death sentence.
- A Knight who betrays the Templars will be punished with death, and all his properties will be confiscated; his family will suffer the same fate.

afterwards, reportedly killed.

Soldiers raiding the Knights Templars' safe houses in 2012 found altars topped with three-foot-high statues of Moreno in golden medieval armour and carrying a sword. A 'Prayer to St. Nazario' circulated, saying: 'Give me holy protection, through St. Nazario, protector of the poorest, knights of the people, St. Nazario, give us life.'

Knights Templar members carry a code book listing fifty-three commandments that members must obey. It is decorated with pictures of Crusaders wearing red crosses. On one occasion, police seized 120 plastic helmets used in ceremonies.

The Knights Templar continued the philanthropic work started by Moreno Gonzáles. 'They help people out by giving them presents like bags of cement,' said an undercover military officer. 'Many people in the area are against authority anyway. Others help the Knights Templar out of fear.' And their activities were still funded by the extortion of protection money from local businesses.

In November 2011 Juan Manuel Orozco Favela, aka *El Gasca*, the *plaza* boss in Morelia, was arrested. One of the Knights Templars' most feared drug bosses, he was charged with kidnapping and killing twenty people on 8 June 2011 in Morelia, together with extortion, trafficking marijuana, providing weapons to comrades in the south of the state and unfurling *narcomantas* attacking *Las Familia*.

Rumours that Moreno Gonzáles had come back from the dead and was still leader of the Knights Templar refused to go away. On the morning of 9 March 2014 any questions were answered once and for all. There was a shoot out between Mexican marines and members of the Knights Templar Cartel in Michoacán, after which news of the death of Moreno Gonzáles was again trumpeted by the Mexican government.

This time there was to be no reprieve. More than 150 heavily armed law-enforcement officers cordoned off the hospital where the autopsy was taking place. Inside was the blood-spattered corpse of Moreno Gonzáles, which duly matched DNA samples and fingerprints on file. There was to be no third coming for Saint Nazario.

Juan Manuel Orozco Favela, aka 'El Gasca', who was arrested in November 2011

Servando Gómez Martínez

All three principal leaders of *La Familia* were the sons of a peasant farmer from Tierra Caliente – 'Hot Land' – that stretches across the borders of Michoacán, Guerrero and Mexico State.

Servando Gómez Martínez was born in the small town of Arteaga in Michoacán in 1966. He was a schoolteacher – hence his nickname '*La Tuta*' or '*El Profe*' – and remained on the federal payroll up to December 2010, though his career in the cartel had begun by then.

Although he was not a religious man like Nazario Moreno González, there was an ideological side to Gómez Martínez. On 15 July 2009, he contacted the local TV phone-in show *Voz y Solución* – 'Voice and Solution' – to praise President Felipe Calderón and the army, who were waging a war against the cartels. The sources of his grievances were the Zetas – mostly drug addicts, he said – and the federal police.

'If someone attacks my father, my mother, or my brother,' he said, 'then they are going to hear from me... Our fight is with the federal police because they are attacking our families.'

In July and August 2009, his mother, brother, girlfriend and nephew were all arrested. That October, Gómez Martínez was indicted by a New York grand jury for drug trafficking.

He offered a truce, even though he was the prime suspect in the torture and murder of twelve police officers found dead earlier that week. Large squads of *La Familia* gunmen had also staged six near-simultaneous attacks on a police station and the accommodation used by federal officials.

'What we want is peace and tranquillity,' he said. 'We want to achieve a national pact. We want the president, Felipe Calderón, to know that we are not his enemies, that we value him, that we are conscientious people.'

He went on to say that *La Familia* had rules and standards, such as kidnapping only politically connected people and 'those who refuse to pay'. The truce was required, he said, because 'we know our work is disliked by the public'. But *La Familia*'s activities were a 'necessary evil', and he wanted, he said, to 'open a dialogue'.

The Minister for the Interior, Fernando Gómez Mont, said that the federal government did not negotiate or make deals with criminal organizations.

Signing off from the phone-in, *La Tuta* said: 'God bless everybody, and let God give us the opportunity to live just a little bit longer. That's all. Thank you.'

After the death of Nazario Moreno González, Servando Gómez Martínez and Enrique Plancarte Solís formed the Knights Templar. On 22 August 2012, *La Tuta* was back in the media again after uploading a video to the website *Blog del Narco*, which aimed to provide information about Mexico's drug war. In the eleven-minute video he allied himself with Che Guevara and Fidel Castro. There were also images of knights and the Mexican flag. He called on the other cartels to oppose Miguel Treviño Morales – Z-40 – head of *Los Zetas*. He also made appeals to President Calderón and the Mexican people, stressing the Templars' 'peaceful credentials' and claiming that they were 'a brotherhood, founded by a set of statutes and codes'. Their function was to preserve the state, keep Mexico free of people causing terror and let the people live in peace.

THE WAR ON DRUGS

LEO XIII.

Drugs such as opium, marijuana, morphine, heroin and cocaine were widely available during the 19th and early 20th centuries. Not only were they prescribed for a range of ailments, they also appeared in tonics and other concoctions generally thought to improve life. Queen Victoria, Robert Louis Stevenson, Émile Zola and President William McKinley all imbibed wine laced with cocaine. Indeed, Pope Leo XIII awarded a Vatican gold medal to the inventor of coca wine, Angelo Mariani. Then there was Coca-Cola, whose original recipe called for a pinch of coca leaves.

George III and his son the Prince Regent took regular draughts of laudanum – opium dissolved in alcohol. It was considered too powerful for children, who were given syrup cordials laced with opium as a cure for

LEFT *Mexican troops come across a marijuana plantation in an area known as The Golden Triangle on the borders of Chihuahua, Sinaloa and Durango states. El Chapo was said to be hiding out in this area*

BELOW LEFT *Pope Leo XIII, who perhaps misguidedly awarded a Vatican gold medal to the inventor of coca wine*

BELOW *Coca cultivation: the dangers of drugs were known when the Spanish first arrived in South America. They claimed that chewing coca leaves was the work of the Devil, but the Catholic Church soon became a leading supplier*

stomachache, teething pains and sleeplessness. Brews such as Godfrey's Cordial, Mrs. Winslow's Soothing Syrup, Mother's Friend or Quietness would put troublesome children into a drug-induced haze.

The dangers of drugs were known back then too. When the Spanish first arrived in South America, they claimed that chewing coca leaves was the work of the Devil. So they taxed coca and soon the Catholic Church, as the leading financial institution in the colonial period, established a virtual monopoly over the coca market in the Andean region.

And it was not just coca. In 1772 one of Mexico's more influential intellectuals, José Antonio Alzate y Ramírez, claimed that marijuana drove its adherents mad, eventually leading them to commune with the Devil.

Opium is native to Turkey. It was unknown in India or China in ancient times. Knowledge of the drug did not reach China until the 7th century, where it was taken as a pill or drunk in a beverage. In that form, it did not produce widespread addiction in Asian societies. However, when Europeans saw Native Americans smoking tobacco in pipes, they began to take opium that way.

Opium smoking was introduced to China in the 17th century and its addictive nature soon became clear. When the Chinese tried to ban its import the British went to war, winning two quick victories in the Opium Wars.

After the Mexican Revolution of 1910–20, opium smoking and the consumption of marijuana were pushed to the fringes of society. Their consumption did not conform to the industrial work ethic that the ruling elite was attempting to impose on the working classes. North of the border it was noted that African-Americans had taken to sniffing cocaine – largely to help them cope with back-breaking labour – and this soon became associated with the danger of physical attacks on the Caucasian population. The result was the Harrison Narcotics Tax Act of 1914, which severely restricted the use and distribution of narcotics.

Opium came to Mexico in 1864, when Chinese workers were brought in to construct the railroads. It was carried by boat from Asia to Mexico's western ports. From there, it was smuggled north across the border into the United States. Initially this was done by the Chinese themselves, but anti-immigrant sentiments demonized the Chinese and restricted their field of action, so the trade was taken over by Mexicans. It became a greater problem when the Philippines government established a monopoly over the cultivation of opium poppies on the islands following the Spanish–American War of 1898.

Outlawing Drugs

In 1909, the United States convened the first conference of the International Opium Commission in Shanghai. The aim was to inhibit the opium trade. Under the resulting treaty, the thirteen participating nations would endeavour to control morphine, cocaine and their salts. The treaty was implemented in 1915 by the United States, China and other nations not then embroiled in the First World War. It came into force globally when it was incorporated into the Versailles Treaty of 1919. Restrictions on hashish and marijuana were added to the Convention in 1925 and went into effect in 1928.

However, thanks to the general lawlessness in Mexico, the trade continued. The United States Border Patrol was established in 1924 and began trying to control who and what crossed the border. But every attempt to clamp down on illegal traffic only resulted in higher profit margins.

Prohibition, which began in 1919, presented Mexican smugglers with a new opportunity – the trafficking of illicit booze. When it was repealed in 1933, the smugglers switched their focus to marijuana and heroin as, unlike coca, marijuana and opium, poppies could be grown and processed in Mexico.

LEFT *The Second Opium War: the French–British army enter Beijing, fighting their way through the Tchao-yant gate in 1860*

RIGHT *Operating out of El Paso, mounted watchmen of the US Immigration Service first patrolled the Mexican border in 1904*

Attempts were made to limit the trade. In 1920 Mexico prohibited the production, sale and recreational use of marijuana and in 1926 opium followed. During this period, in 1923, the importation of all narcotics was prohibited and measures were implemented to limit the sale of alcohol to the United States. There was a 'dry zone' 50 miles (80 km) wide along the northern border and an airfield was built at Ciudad Juárez for its surveillance.

The laws were tightened again in 1925, following a cross-border agreement, and in 1927 the export of Mexican marijuana and heroin was banned outright, which meant the whole narcotics industry was now outlawed. Attempts to stamp it out completely were undermined by official involvement in the drugs trade, but these activities

were thwarted by the introduction of the United States Marihuana Tax Act in 1937, which effectively criminalized the non-medicinal use of marijuana in the US.

However, the production of drugs in Mexico was soon given a boost. During the Second World War the United States government needed morphine to treat its wounded servicemen, but the flow of heroin from Europe had been halted, together with the supply of Asian morphine. As a result, the growing of poppies in Sinaloa was encouraged by the US.

Mexican marijuana growers also took advantage of the disruption of traditional overseas routes to cash in on the growing post-war demand. Poverty in the northern states of Mexico meant that farmers could earn more by growing poppies than by producing corn.

Other illegal drugs were brought in by Japanese fishing boats, with the contraband hidden inside fish. That way, it could easily be shipped into the United States.

Communism in Our Backyard

During the Cold War, the state department complained about the drug-smuggling activities of the DFS – *Dirección Federal de Seguridad* or 'National Security Directorate' – but the CIA turned a blind eye to the situation. Drug traffickers furnished the CIA with information about suspected Communist groups and profits from cocaine trafficking helped fund right-wing coups in Argentina and Bolivia. While the DFS repressed the left wing and supplied information on the activities of Soviet, Eastern Bloc and Cuban officials in Mexico, the United States would tolerate a little drug smuggling. Sometimes, the CIA was actively involved.

The small independent traffickers who had operated before the war now sought the political cover that the larger organizations could offer. Domestically, anti-trafficking operations also became a cover for political repression and gave the government the excuse to spy on its own citizens.

The Mexican Army was also called into the fray. With little threat of foreign invasion, in 1948 it was employed in the *Gran Campaña* – 'Great Campaign' – against drugs. However, despite being ostensibly tasked to eradicate the trade, it was also charged with defending the interests of those who profited from it. While the army burned the plantations of the smaller growers, the larger operations could offer sufficient bribes to be left alone.

Mexican troops destroy opium poppies. During World War II, the US encouraged Mexico to grow them to make up for a shortfall in supplies of morphine. Now Mexico produces 7 per cent of the world's total supply

Small glass pipes called 'straight shooters' are used to smoke crack cocaine, with a small piece of wire wool acting as filter.
Mexicans used to act as intermediaries for the Colombian cartels in cocaine smuggling, but now they produce their own crops

The Mafia also took advantage of Mexico's two-thousand-mile border with the United States to smuggle heroin. But in the late 1960s the government in Turkey – where most opiates destined for the United States originated – banned the growing of poppies and the French Connection through Marseilles was broken. Given its proximity to the United States and its corrupt political class, Mexico was the obvious source for new supplies.

The Hippy Era

During the 1960s, the smoking of marijuana among young people in the United States became endemic. Mexico again became the principal supplier. By 1975, 8 per cent of the heroin and 95 per cent of the marijuana consumed in the United States came from Mexico. Demand was growing and the price was stable, so there was little point in farmers growing traditional crops such as corn, beans, almonds and vanilla. The United States Bureau of the Budget noted that marijuana offered individual farmers up to forty times the income that any legitimate crop could provide.

In 1969 President Richard Nixon authorized Operation Intercept, which attempted to halt the flow of marijuana over the Mexican border. He feared the upswelling of the anti-war and civil rights movements, which seemed to be conducted by people who smoked the drug. Soldiers in Vietnam were also smoking dope and deserting in ever increasing numbers.

All vehicles crossing the border were stopped and searched. But President Díaz Ordaz had not been consulted and the Mexicans were outraged. This also hampered legal exports, damaging the Mexican economy. In another attempt to handle the problem, President Nixon established the Drug Enforcement Administration in 1973.

Meanwhile President Díaz Ordaz was having problems with dope-smoking students himself. Somewhere between thirty and three hundred students were massacred in Tlatelolco in 1968, only ten days before the opening of the Summer Olympics in Mexico City.

There was trouble in the countryside too, where a number of armed guerrilla groups sprang up. Lucio Cabañas Barrientos led an army of two hundred activists in Guerrero. In 1971 Días Ordaz's successor President Luis Echeverría Álvarez dispatched 12,000 troops to the area.

Between 1971 and 1974, there was a series of kidnappings and bombings across Mexico. By the time Cabañas Barrientos was killed in 1974, there were 24,000 soldiers in Guerrero – a third of the Mexican army. Martial law was in force and some 650 people 'disappeared' in the municipality of Atoyac de Álvarez alone.

In the *guerra sucia* – or 'dirty war' – propaganda associated political activism with drug trafficking. This gave the DFS the opportunity to crack down on trafficking – not to arrest the *narcos*, but to profit from it themselves. Meanwhile its paramilitary wing, *La Brigada Blanca*, could eliminate dissidents on the pretext that they were criminals.

Eradicating the Crops

Business was booming. In the *triángulo crítico* or *triángulo dorado* – the 'critical' or 'Golden Triangle' in the northern states of Sinaloa, Durango and Chihuahua – some 600,000 square kilometres were being used to grow marijuana and poppies. Plans were laid to eradicate the crops in Operation Condor. Five thousand troops and 350 members of the Federal Judicial Police would be sent into the Golden Triangle. The United States supplied seventy-six aircraft and invested $150 million in the operation and some thirty United States agents were sent to oversee the campaign and identify targets. For the first time United States agents would have a formal presence in Mexico.

The herbicide Paraquat would be sprayed from the air on to the fields, despite the dire effects of the defoliant Agent Orange in Vietnam. Soon marijuana containing 44,000 times the safe level of Paraquat was reaching the United States.

In its first three years, Operation Condor succeeded in destroying most of the marijuana and opium fields in the Golden Triangle, but it increased the 'cartelization' of the trade. Peasant farmers who had previously taken up arms to defend their fields from soldiers had no chance against aerial spraying. However, the bigger operators had the resources to plant smaller plots in remote areas, where they were difficult to detect. Nevertheless, by 1979 the amount of heroin entering the United States had almost halved. This meant that the price rose and the quality dropped.

With 70 per cent of the marijuana fields in Mexico out of action, Colombian growers benefited by supplying the undiminished demand in the American market. In Mexico, some better-off traffickers even defended their plantations by shooting at the crop-spraying planes. The smuggling industry rewarded the ruthless and those

President Nixon established the Drug Enforcement Administration in 1973 as part of his bid to keep a lid on rebellious activities in the US

who had the money to buy off the DFS, the police, the politicians and the military. For example, drug lord Alberto Sicilia Falcón used his political connections in the CIA and Mexican intelligence to divert the government eradication programme from his own plantation to those of his competitors. In some cases, the planes that were supposed to be spraying herbicide were actually spraying water and fertilizer on the crop. Officials would go joyriding on planes, or use them to shake down growers who wanted protection from the eradication programme. Meanwhile the DFS was using its own fleet of six hundred tankers to transport marijuana across

Silver or Lead

The cartels' response to the war on drugs was *Plata o Plomo* – 'Silver or Lead'. Either you got on the cartel's payroll or they killed you. The director of the federal police force in Tijuana, Ernest Ibarra, had been in office for just twenty-nine days when he scolded his men by saying that they were so corrupt that they weren't just friends with the traffickers, they were their servants. Two days later, he was machine-gunned, along with two other officers, in Mexico City. An army officer was implicated in his murder.

Baja State prosecutor, Godin Gutiérrez, was killed in front of his Tijuana home in January 1997. He had helped the DEA identify several

assassins in the Arellano-Félix Organization. Gutiérrez was shot over a hundred times and then run over repeatedly by a car.

In another effort to discourage police corruption, President Zedillo sent a young police reformer, José Patiño, to clean up Tijuana's ranks. For his own safety, he lived across the border in San Diego. A DEA agent who had investigated the cartel for years once said that Patiño was the only Mexican police officer he had ever worked with who appeared to be honest. But in April 2000 Patiño, special prosecutor Oscar Pompa and army captain Rafael Torres were lured into a trap by two Mexican federal police officers, trained by the United States to be part of a new, 'clean' anti-drug unit. Patiño and his aides were found in a ditch the next day with almost every bone in their bodies broken and their heads crushed by an industrial press. One policeman said their remains resembled bags of ice cubes.

United States Immigration and Naturalization Service inspector José Olvera, who manned the Tijuana–San Ysidro border crossing, also took the *plata*. He pleaded guilty to taking nearly $90,000 in bribes to allow cartel shipments through. Olvera said he had complied with the cartel's wishes because they had threatened to kidnap his five-year-old son – a common tactic.

'If relatively well paid United States agents aren't immune,' said one Mexican prosecutor, 'how can we expect Mexican police to be?'

the border, bribing Mexican and United States border officials so that the illicit cargo would arrive in Phoenix and Los Angeles unhindered. After all, those involved in the eradication programme had $150 million supplied by the United States government to play with.

Those outside this charmed circle of corruption suffered. Growing legal crops had barely provided a living before Operation Condor started. Now legitimate farmers found that their health and their harvests were failing. They had no choice but to flee to the city, adding to urban poverty, or cross the border into the United States as illegal immigrants. Those that could afford it paid a tax of $60 on every kilo of contraband they produced – $20 went to the military leader in the area, $20 to the DFS and $20 to the federal police. People lost all respect for authority.

Corruption

The DEA noticed that every top trafficker they arrested was carrying a DFS badge. This allowed him to carry a machine gun, install wiretap devices and interrogate detainees. DFS agents would also protect shipments. By tapping into Mexican police radio, they could access United States police surveillance messages and ensure safe passage across the border.

In the 1980s, the 'war on drugs' became part of United States domestic and foreign policy. The South Florida Drug Task Force concentrated on shipments of Colombian marijuana and cocaine being landed on the coast for distribution through Miami. Seizures of cocaine rose from two tons in 1981 to a hundred tons in 1989, but this only upped the price and boosted drug trafficking through Mexico.

In May 1984 journalist Manuel Buendía Tellezgirón wrote that the Secretary of the Interior, the director of the PJF's anti-drug enforcement programme and the former head of the PJF all had close ties with the drug traffickers. He was soon silenced. On 30 May, he was shot five times in the back at point blank range. DFS agent Juan Rafael Moro Ávila, a relative of former president Manuel Ávila Camacho, was eventually jailed for the murder of Buendía, along with DFS chief José Antonio Zorrilla Pérez. Following the investigation into the murder of Enrique 'Kiki' Camarena, which also implicated Zorrilla Pérez, the DFS was closed down.

Four years later, its role was taken over by the *Centro de Investigación y Seguridad Nacional* (CISEN) – National Security and Investigation Center. Little changed, though the state's control of the drugs trade was slightly weakened. Any resistance to the drug traffickers was overcome by the CIA and Colonel Oliver North, who used them to get money and guns to the Contras in Nicaragua. Caro Quintero's ranch in Veracruz even became a training centre for the Contras. In exchange, the cartels – particularly the Guadalajara Cartel – were given free access to United States cities such as Los Angeles, where dealers bought Colombian cocaine from Mexican traffickers and processed it into crack. While the United States and Mexican governments were ostensibly spending millions of dollars on stamping out the drugs trade, their intelligence and security services were funding it.

In 1988, a rigged election brought Carlos Salinas de Gortari to power as president. He began the process of wholesale privatization and deregulation. The North American Free Trade Agreement (NAFTA) came into force in 1994, reducing trade restrictions between Mexico, the United States and Canada. During the negotiations, members of the DEA and the United States Customs Service were specifically prohibited from raising the subject of drug trafficking. Soon 75 per cent of the cocaine entering the United States was coming through Mexico. Mexico was also providing marijuana, heroin and methamphetamine of its own, and United States banks were laundering around $250 billion a year of criminal earnings. Even President Salinas' brother Raúl, who had an estimated $300 million tucked away in offshore accounts, was accused of having links with the cartels. He replied that the benefits of political and financial nepotism were such that he hardly needed to become involved in drug trafficking.

Ernesto Zedillo Ponce de León became president in 1994. His contribution to the war on drugs was to give the military a greater role. The collapse of the Soviet Union in 1991 had ended the Cold War, but in 1994 an army of insurgents calling themselves Zapatistas – after the revolutionary Emiliano Zapata – appeared, renewing the justification for repression. They assassinated presidential candidate Luis Donaldo Colosio and foreign investment fled.

In 1996, President Zedillo appointed General Jesús

Gutiérrez Rebollo to lead the anti-drug agency *Instituto Nacional para el Combate a las Drogas*. Bill Clinton's drug czar General Barry McCaffrey told *The New York Times* that Gutiérrez Rebollo was a man of 'unquestioned integrity'. The Pentagon offered $28 million in aid, soon increased to $78 million, and agreed to train 1,100 Mexican soldiers.

The Special Forces Airmobile Group (GAFE) – a Mexican quick response military entity, who trained at the School of the Americas at Fort Benning, Georgia – were given a specific anti-drugs role. However, by 1997 they had not made one cocaine seizure or arrested a single major criminal. Instead, some members had been arrested for trafficking cocaine, while others had been involved in torturing 'suspects', though no information was forthcoming. Two years later, some thirty of them left to form *Los Zetas*, taking their weapons with them.

It is ironic that Gutiérrez Rebollo directed the arrest of Carrillo Fuentes in 1989, because he would later be imprisoned because of his relationship with the drug baron. However, the charges against Carrillo Fuentes were dropped and he was released from the Reclusorio Sur prison in Mexico City in 1990. The director of the prison, Adrián Carrera, remained on Carrillo Fuentes' payroll and went on to become director of the PJF.

Carrera was arrested in 1998 and given the opportunity to turn state's evidence rather than face a long prison term. He testified that he had delivered $2 million to Mario Ruiz Massieu, the brother of assassinated deputy attorney general José Francisco Ruiz Massieu. Mario committed suicide after $17 million was found in his bank accounts in the United States. Raúl Salinas was convicted of masterminding José Francisco, but the conviction was overturned on appeal.

In 1997 information emerged about Gutiérrez Rebollo. For instance, he had conducted a three-month operation against the Arellano-Félix brothers, paid for by Carrillo Fuentes. It was also found that he was living in an apartment that he could scarcely afford on a general's wages. Carrillo Fuentes was paying for it. Gutiérrez Rebollo was sentenced to thirty-one years for abusing his position and using the military in a criminal enterprise. Later, he was given another forty years for aiding Carrillo Fuentes.

Gutiérrez Rebollo was not the only high-ranking Mexican to abuse his position. At a hearing, Gutiérrez said that President Zedillo's father-in-law had business links to the Colima Cartel. But the prosecution firmly denied this. In any case, the arraignment of the odd scapegoat like Gutiérrez was enough to earn Mexico its anti-drug certification. This meant that the $64 million in surveillance equipment and satellite-guided UH-60 Blackhawk helicopters provided by President Clinton could be diverted to cracking down on the Zapatistas rather than drug traffickers. Hundreds of suspected Zapatista supporters were killed by the army and paramilitary death squads.

LEFT *The funeral of forty-five Tzotsil Mayan Indians, including fifteen children, killed at Acteal by paramilitary death squads after forces surrounded a Catholic chapel in December 1997*

BELOW *Vincente Fox was elected president in 2000 and promised to clean up corruption (like so many Mexican politicians before him)*

In 1997, in the village of Acteal in Chiapas, a paramilitary squad called *Máscara Roja* – 'Red Mask' – massacred a gathering of the Catholic pacifist group called *Las Abejas* – 'The Bees' – killing forty-nine, including twenty-one women, fifteen children and four unborn babies. The pregnant women's stomachs were cut open with machetes and the babies inside were yanked out and their heads dashed against rocks to kill *las semilla* – 'the seed'. It was part of an organized strategy to terrorize the rural population.

Change of Power

Until the year 2000, the *Partido Revolucionario Institucional* (PRI) – Institutional Revolutionary Party – had been in power for seventy-one years. Then the *Partido Acción Nacional* (PAN) – National Action Party – under Vicente Fox was elected. Fox promised to clean up corruption, but he was up against some stiff opposition. That year, *Forbes* magazine listed Joaquín '*El Chapo*'

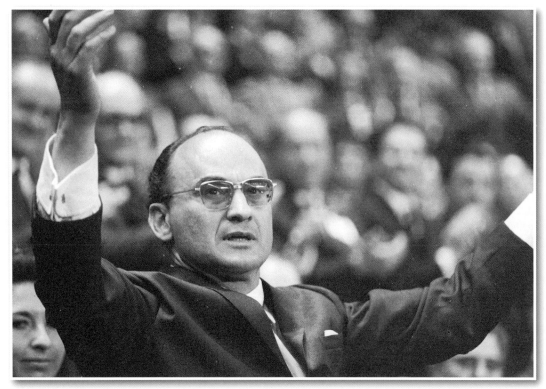

LEFT *Luis Echeverría Álvarez became one of Fox's advisors, but included generals from the dirty war among his cohorts*

RIGHT *A man lies dead in the streets of a small town not far from Monterrey, another victim of drug-cartel gunmen*

Guzmán Loera as the sixtieth most powerful person on the planet. It has been alleged that his escape from Puente Grande maximum security prison just one month after the PAN came to power was due to a $20 million bribe he had given to Fox when he was governor of Guanajuato.

Though *cambio* – 'change' – had been promised, no changes took place. The old parties maintained a majority in the legislature, preventing any fundamental reform. This left a power vacuum that could be filled by the narcos, who became increasingly independent of government and consequently more powerful. Luis Echeverría Álvarez – former Secretary of the Interior in the Días Ordaz administration, who on top of everything else had overseen the massacre at Tlatelolco – became one of President Fox's closest advisers. His loyal cohorts, including generals from the dirty war, also joined the administration. Meanwhile, a change in power at the provincial level disrupted the old *plaza* system, promoting new turf wars.

In an attempt to boost the legitimate economy, *maquiladoras* had been established along Mexico's northern border. These were foreign-owned factories designed to feed the United States market with inexpensive manufactured goods by exploiting cheap Mexican labour. They received a boost with the signing of NAFTA, which increased the cross-border traffic – something the enterprising narco-traffickers could also take advantage of.

The population of the border towns swelled, but when demand fell after Chinese manufactured goods began to dominate the United States market the resulting unemployment provided the cartels with willing foot soldiers.

Migrants wanting to get across the border provided another revenue stream for the cartels. They were also taken advantage of by the police, who arrested them and forced them to sign false drug-dealing confessions – allowing the authorities to claim that they were winning the war on drugs.

In 2003, the offices of the *Fiscalía Especializada en Atención de Delitos contra la Salud* (FEADS) – the federal agency set up in 1997 to investigate corruption and organized crime – were raided. FEADS agents had been seizing drugs during raids and selling them. In one office, five tons of undeclared marijuana was found. Six senior officers were arrested for drugs and arms smuggling, kidnapping or leaking information to the Sinaloa Cartel. Thirty-five other members, including the senior intelligence officer, were arrested or fired. Around the

same time Mexico's liaison officer with Interpol and two senior federal police commanders were also arrested for tipping off the cartels.

The FEADS had its successes though. As well as selling drugs, its agents had killed Benjamin and Ramón Arellano-Félix, *El Chapo*'s major rivals. But in spite of the Archbishop of Durango declaring that he knew where *El Chapo* lived, no one went to arrest him.

In December 2009, Felipe Calderón became president in another dubious election. He initiated a new phase in the war on drugs, fully committing the military by putting 50,000 troops on the streets. But they were betrayed from the beginning. After the scandal at the FEADS, the organization had been replaced by the SIEDO – the Assistant Attorney General's Office for Special Investigations on Organized Crime. Its head

was Noé Ramírez Mandujano, who was tipping off the Sinaloa Cartel for a payment of $450,000 a month. In 2008, he resigned after SIEDO had made a suspiciously small number of arrests. He went on to become Mexico's representative to the United Nations Office on Drugs and Crime. Later he was arrested and jailed.

In 2009 the entire municipal authority of the town of Tancítaro, Michoacán resigned after declaring that the increased incidence of kidnapping, executions and forced disappearances had made their job too dangerous. Since Felipe Calderón had become president in December 2006 there had been 39,000 deaths related to drug cartel violence. Mexico's National Human Rights Commission had registered more than five thousand people missing or disappeared and there were around nine thousand corpses yet to be identified. According to the testimony of one *sicario*, there are at least a hundred clandestine *narcofosas* – mass graves – containing thousands of bodies yet to be discovered. And public displays of violence have become more frequent. The number of bodies dumped with signs of torture and accompanied by *narcomantas* has soared, and videos showing the torture and killing of members of rival cartels are regularly posted on YouTube.

President Barack Obama signed off $700 million to improve security in Mexico. Another $450 million was allocated for military training in 2010 and the United States continues to supply high-tech equipment. Between 2007 and 2011, the national institutions dedicated to fighting the drugs trade had their budgets increased by 77 per cent. But still the number of homicides related to narco-trafficking climbed from 2,119 in 2006 to 8,837 in 2011, peaking at 11,583 in 2010.

But drug traffic did not shrink significantly during this time and the killers continued to act with impunity. Less than 5 per cent of drug-related murders were investigated and less than one per cent of criminal investigations were related to the drugs trade. In fact, it is estimated that 99 per cent of crimes in Mexico go unpunished. Nevertheless, during the Calderón administration the federal government claimed that half of the top narco *capos* had been killed or captured.

Meanwhile reported cases of kidnapping soared by 188 per cent, car theft by 123 per cent, extortion by 101 per cent, homicide by 96 per cent and theft with violence by 42 per cent. According to Human Rights Watch, in 2010–11 the police and the military were responsible for 170 cases of torture, 39 forced disappearances and 24 extra-judicial executions.

All merchants in Cancún pay for protection and if a restaurateur does so he gets no visits from health or tax inspectors. In Monterrey all street vendors are controlled by the cartels. The cartels 'represent justice' in entire zones of Michoacán and control all federal toll roads. Around half a million people work either directly or indirectly for the cartels, which have an annual budget of $25 billion – or $40 billion if you include money laundering. The United States government was forced to bail out banks connected to drugs money laundering in the 2008 banking crisis.

The money spent combating the cartels does not nearly match the amount at the disposal of the drug lords. What

money there is goes to the army, whose low-paid recruits regularly desert, taking their weapons with them, and the police – it is estimated that some 62 per cent of the force are linked to, or controlled by, the cartels and 57 per cent of their weapons are used in illegal activities. Instead of destroying the drug plantations, the police and the military work for the traffickers, protecting the crops. Indeed, the cartels recruit directly from the army and the police force, because the new recruits will have already been trained to use firearms, are disciplined and physically fit and will kill if ordered to do so. One *sicario* claimed that at the end of his training at the police academy at least fifty of his two hundred classmates joined criminal organizations. The Mexican taxpayer is paying to train *sicarios*.

Those that stay in the force are little better. By 2005, 1,500 members of the Federal Agency of Investigation were under investigation and 457 had been charged with colluding with organized crime. There were also allegations that its head, Genaro García Luna, had links to the Sinaloa Cartel. In less than three years as Secretary of Public Security his acquisitions totalled seventeen times his salary.

Meanwhile, 174 police officers and politicians were murdered between December 2006 and August 2011, including 83 police chiefs, 32 municipal presidents and five political candidates. It has been said that this is not a war on drugs but a war for drugs. And the cartels' global reach is growing. They are now importing heroin from Afghanistan and exporting drugs to Argentina.

Clearly President Calderón's *guerra al narco* had failed. Many Mexicans followed the poet Javier Sicilia on to the street in his *No Más Sangre* – 'No More Blood' – protest movement. His son had been tortured and killed by a drug cartel in Cuernavaca. The anti-drug *Indignados* – Outraged – movement demanded Calderón's removal.

On 1 December 2012, he was replaced by Enrique Peña Nieto. However, President Peña Nieto is a member of the PRI, the party that ruled Mexico from the Revolution until 2000 when the cartels grew to prominence. What were the chances he would turn back the tide?

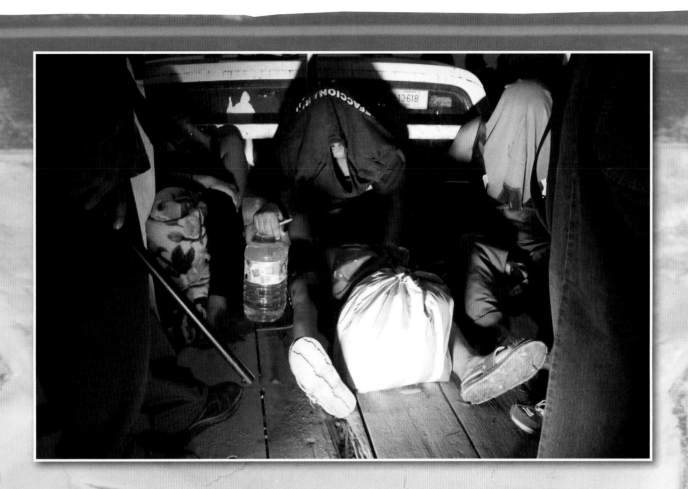

Auto Defensa

In January 2013, photojournalist Ross McDonnell travelled into the mountains of Guerrero to report on the *Auto Defensa* movement – autonomous uprisings of *campesinos* who had been pushed to breaking point by the cartels and were now determined to regain control of their towns and villages. This began on 5 January in Ayutla de los Libres, a town of around 30,000 people, when the local *comesario* was kidnapped. The residents armed themselves and closed the roads in and out of the town. Patrols soon found the *comesario* and freed him. His captors were taken prisoner.

This was not technically a vigilante action. Under the Mexican constitution, indigenous communities in some parts of the country are allowed to form their own police force. So the locals kicked out both the municipal and federal police. Masked and wielding shotguns and machetes, they began clearing the streets of criminals. Crime was cut by 90 per cent and Guerrero's governor, Ángel Heladio Aguirre Rivero, praised their efforts.

Some are critical of what has become the *Policía Communitaria*, saying that they are violating human rights and denying the accused due legal process. At one time, some sixty prisoners were being held in a makeshift prison and paraded in front of crowds to shame them. However, the stout resistance of the residents of Ayutla de los Libres has inspired other towns and villages in Guerrero to take up arms against the cartels.

FURTHER READING

Amexica: War Along the Borderline by Ed Vulliamy, Vintage, London, 2010

Bordering on Chaos: Guerrillas, Stockbrokers, Politicians, and Mexico's Road to Prosperity by Andres Oppenheimer, Little, Brown, Boston, 1996

Bribes, Bullets, and Intimidation by Julie Marie Bunck and Michael Ross Fowler, Pennsylvania University Press, Philadelphia, 2012

Cartel: The Coming Invasion of Mexico's Drug Wars by Sylvia Longmire, Palgrave Macmillan, New York, 2011

Cartels At War: Mexico's Drug-Fueled Violence and the Threat to U.S. National Security by Paul Rexton Kan, Potomac Books, Washington, D.C., 2012

Dead Biker: Inside the Violent World of the Mexican Drug Cartels by Jerry Langton, John Wiley & Sons, Mississauga, Ontario, 2012

The Dead Women of Juárez: Murder and Abduction in a Mexican Border Town by Sam Hawken, Serpent's Tail, London, 2011

Drug Crazy: How We Got Into This Mess and How We Can Get Out by Mike Gray, Random House, New York, 1998

Drug War Mexico: Politics, Neoliberalism and Violence in the New Narcoeconomy by Peter Watt and Roberto Zepeda, Zed Books, London and New York, 2012

Drug War Zone: Frontline Dispatches from the Streets of El Paso and Juárez by Howard Campbell, University of Texas Press, Austin, 2009

El Narco: The Bloody Rise of the Mexican Drug Cartels by Ioan Grillo, Bloomsbury, London, 2012

El Sicario: Confessions of a Cartel Hit Man edited by Molly Molloy and Charles Bowden, William Heinemann, London, 2011

The Executioner's Men: Los Zetas, Rogue Soldiers, Criminal Entrepreneurs and the Shadow State They Created by George W. Grayson and Samuel Logan, Transaction Publishers, New Brunswick, New Jersey, 2012

Home Grown: Marijuana and the Origins of Mexico's War on Drugs by Isaac Campos, University of North Carolina Press, Chapel Hill, North Carolina, 2012

The Last Narco by Malcolm Beith, Grove Press, New York, 2010

Mexico: Narco-Violence and a Failed State? by George W. Grayson, Transaction Publishers, New Brunswick, New Jersey, 2010

Mexico's Security Failure: Collapse into Criminal Violence edited by Paul Kenny and Mónica Serrano with Arturo Sotomayor, Routledge, New York, 2012

Narcos Over the Border: Gangs, Cartels and Mercenaries edited by Robert J. Bunker, Routledge, London and New York, 2011

Organized Crime and Democratic Governability: Mexico and the US–Mexican Borderlands edited by John Bailey and Roy Godson, University of Pittsburgh Press, Pittsburgh, 2000

Tequila Sunset by Sam Hawken, Serpent's Tail, London, 2012

Whiteout: The CIA, Drugs and the Press by Alexander Cockburn and Jeffrey St. Clair, Verso, London and New York, 1998

PICTURE CREDITS

Corbis: 6 (Keith Dannemiller), 8 (STRINGER/MEXICO/Reuters), 21b (Reuters), 23 (Tony Comiti), 26 (Sergio Dorantes/Sygma), 28-29 (Sergio Dorantes/Sygma), 38t (Jazmín Adrián/Demotix), 38b (HO/Reuters), 42 (SEMAR/Xinhua Press), 43 (MARIO GUZMAN/epa), 45 (EDGARD GARRIDO/Reuters), 46-47 (DANIEL AGUILAR/Reuters), 49 (Reuters), 51 (REUTERS/El Debate de Sinaloa), 52 (STRINGER/MEXICO/Reuters), 54 (Alex Cruz/epa), 55 (Mario Guzmán/epa), 57t (HENRY ROMERO/Reuters), 57b (Jazmin Adrian/Demotix), 59 (Xinhua Press), 60 (STR/epa), 62 (HO/Reuters), 64 (MARIO GUZMAN/epa), 69 (Andrew Lichtenstein/Sygma), 70b (Pat Cunningham/Sygma), 72 (STRINGER/MEXICO/Reuters), 73 (MARIO GUZMAN/epa), 74 (STRINGER/MEXICO/Reuters), 75 (Reuters), 77 (HO/Reuters), 81 (JUAN CEDILLO/epa), 82 (STRINGER/MEXICO/Reuters), 84 (MARIO GUZMAN/epa), 85 (STRINGER/MEXICO/Reuters), 86 (AHMAD MASOOD/Reuters), 87 (STR/epa), 88 (Guillermo Arias/Xinhua Press), 89 (MARIO GUZMAN/epa), 90 (Janet Jarman), 94 (POOL/Xinhua Press), 96-7 (Radius Images), 100 (Claudio Cruz/Xinhua Press), 102 (ETTORE FERRARI/epa), 104 (STRINGER/MEXICO/Reuters), 106 (Enrique Perez Huerta/Demotix), 112 (Reuters), 115, 118 (Allan Barnes/Sygma), 119 (Sergio Dorantes/Sygma), 121 (Pedro Kristian Lopez/Demotix), 123 (STRINGER/epa)

Getty: 16 (Time & Life Pictures), 18 (AFP), 41 (AFP), 48, 63 (AFP), 70t (AFP), 76 (AFP), 98t (MCT via Getty Images), 108t (MCT via Getty Images)

Press Association: 11l (La Jorada), 14, 24t (Reforma), 25 (David J. Phillip), 30 (HO), 34t (MIGUEL ZUBIETA), 34b, 36 (Miguel Tovar/AP), 37bl (DARIO LOPEZ-MILLS), 37bc, 37br (SSP-HO), 50 (Mexico Attorney General's Office), 67 (Sol De Culiacan), 68 (Raymundo Ruiz), 71 (STR/ Mexico Attorney General's Office), 80 (Antonio Sierra), 83 (Miguel Tovar), 92 (Miguel Tovar), 98b (Marco Ugarte), 101 (Marco Ugarte), 120

Shutterstock: 2-5, 11r, 12, 17 (Daniel Korzeniewski), 20-21, 24, 33, 39, 56, 58, 66 (Frontpage), 78, 79 (Randy Miramontez), 103, 108b, 109, 110, 111, 114, 116, 124

David Woodroffe: 10

INDEX